How *Not* to be a Domestic Goddess

DEBORAH ROSS is an award-winning columnist and interviewer for the *Independent*, *Spectator* and *Daily Mail*. She lives in north London with her partner and son who have never been any support whatsoever, but that is the cross she has to bear. Considered one of Britain's funniest columnists, this is her first venture into book form.

How *Not* to be a Domestic Goddess

Deborah Ross

with illustrations by Mary Leunig

P

PROFILE BOOKS

This paperback edition published in 2008

First published in Great Britain in 2007 by
PROFILE BOOKS LTD
3A Exmouth House
Pine Street
London ECIR OJH
www.profilebooks.com

10 9 8 7 6 5 4 3 2 1

Designed by Nicky Barneby @ Barneby Ltd
Set in 12.5/15pt Mrs Eaves
Printed and bound in Great Britain by CPI Bookmarque, CR0 4TD

Formerly published as *Always go to Bed on an Argument*

A CIP catalogue record for this book is available from the British Library.

ISBN 978 1 86197 891 2

For Geraint, Nye, Georgia and Stells, who have been no help whatsoever but that is the cross I have to bear.

Contents

Introduction

This is a book for Non-Domestic Goddesses so if you are not a Non-Domestic Goddess then: go away, we do not want you. Further, you should be aware that we do have the most exactingly low standards and will not accept just anybody. We recently, for example, had to reject Anthea Turner on the grounds she'd appeared on TV saying you simply cannot have too many wicker baskets for storage. 'Anthea,' we had to tell her, 'do put a sock in it.' Note it is a sock, not a pair of socks, and much less a matching pair of socks. As a Non-Domestic Goddess, it's best to be realistic about what is likely to be to hand and what is not. As a Non-Domestic Goddess, there is every chance you haven't seen a matching pair of socks since 1976, and even then you may have dreamt it.

So, maybe you think you are a Non-Domestic

Goddess. Maybe you, too, have defrosted a chicken in the bath, swung a child's swimming trunks round your head in an attempt to dry them just before the next lesson, wept while reading *Elle Decoration*, calling out, 'How do you get to live like this?' and have, at some time or another, suffered from a full-blown attack of Cometitis, the deadly sickness that strikes once you get caught up in that dark underworld called Customer Services. You might also fret about this thing called a 'lifestyle': what is it exactly? And where can I get one if I suspect I'm without? As for Ikea, you would love it if only it didn't make you quite so faint and dizzy: so many veneers, so little time!

Certainly, any of the above would be a good start, we'll give you that. But the true Non-Domestic Goddess allows her exacting low standards to seep into all areas of her life. She tries to keep up with fashion and yearns to live in Bodenland, where women drape fetchingly on driftwood and children companionably rock-pool while keeping their sun hats *on*. She yearns, too, for a 'sexy sweater dress' that doesn't retain the shape of her bottom after the very first sit-down, so making her look about as sexy as a badly-knitted baboon. On reflection, no wonder they don't allow her into Bodenland. Be honest: would you?

She also, of course, tries to maintain a beauty

regime, tries to love the skin she is in but, after looking at it from all angles, always concludes: 'Nope, sorry, no can do.' Further, when Jane Fonda appears on TV, advertising some face cream and saying, 'Not bad for 68, huh?' the true Non-Domestic Goddess will always want to shout back, 'Come on, love. Get a grip. You looked one hell of a lot better as Barbarella.' The Non-Domestic Goddess figures someone has to say so, and what's wrong with growing old anyway? Why is the older woman always treated as just so useless when it's simply not true? Two older women, for example, can make very nice bookends, and bookends are always handy. Ask anyone.

Naturally, at the start of every New Year the Non-Domestic Goddess will embark on a 'New You' health and fitness programme. And why not? It's only about tweaking who she already is to become someone else entirely while setting the alarm for the early morning run she is never going to go on. She may even be a fan of Dr Gillian McKeith and her particular way of bullying fat people on television until they cry. She may even have written her a fan letter along the following lines: 'Assuming *your* poo smells of pot-pourri, can you tell me why I've yet to see it in hotel lobbies or the entrances to stately homes? Thanking you . . . etc., etc.'

Of course, the Non-Domestic Goddess loves her

children, even though they are very annoying and she is somehow always to blame for the fit of their swimming goggles — 'They're leaking; now they're too tight!' She has sat through many school plays even though she knows that there will always be one child who knows all the lines and will shout them into the faces of those that don't (and they call this quality entertainment?) She also knows her children shouldn't watch too much television, but what the hell, particularly when the alternative might involve doing glittery stuff with glue or playing a board game — eat the dice; it'll be over in no time; it's the only way. And she understands teenagers, or at least how best to embarrass them. Wearing a push-up bra to parents' evening usually does it, as does wearing something tight in leather. The two together, she has discovered, do the job spectacularly well.

As for the secret to a happy marriage, no, a Non-Domestic Goddess does not know that. She accepts, though, that 'give and take' is often the key. As such, she will always offer to compromise, and will even go along with it for a bit before revealing, 'Hey, I was only joking.' She does, though, know the secret to keeping an average marriage limping along and it is this: always go to bed on an argument; that way, you can resume hostilities first thing without wasting any valuable time.

Introduction

Think you make the grade? Think you can cut it as a proper Non-Domestic Goddess? If so, and you believe as we do that, as a woman's work is never done (so what's the point in even making a start?) then take the first step and join the Non-Domestic Goddess Club of Great Britain (NDGC (GB)). You can be sure of a warm welcome as well as a nice cup of Nescafé made by running the mug under the hot tap. There may even be cake, shop-bought of course, but perhaps bashed about a bit to look homemade. There are no flies on the true Non-Domestic Goddess, probably because they are all in her fruit bowl and sometimes even in her flour . . .

1

House and
Home

'As with the commander of an army, so it is with the mistress of the house,' writes Mrs Beeton in her *Book of Household Management*. A good housewife, she continues, must be clean, frugal, efficient and, most importantly, an early riser. 'When the mistress is an early riser,' she says, 'it is almost certain that the house will be orderly and well-managed.' So it is essential to rise early, which may mean getting up before lunch. Anytime after lunch is obscene unless you can (a) get away with it and (b) do one of those convincing 'What? I've been up for *ages*' voices on the phone. This kind of housewife is probably not a good housewife, but that's OK, because she can always join the Non-Domestic Goddess Club of Great Britain. Our manifesto is printed below not just for your information, but so you can later spill coffee all over it before throwing it out by mistake.

The Non-Domestic Goddess Club (GB)

Welcome to the Non-Domestic Goddess Club (GB). This is the largest organisation in the UK for those who cannot only do that 'What? I've been up for *ages*' voice but probably also somehow have very old ice-lollies embedded in the iced-up walls of their freezer. The Club, founded at some time or another but no one can say when exactly as the members forgot to write it on the calendar, operates under the slogan 'Nature abhors a vacuum and so do we'. The Club also, by the way, abhors the Dyson. This was decided at the last AGM on the grounds that just because it is red and funky and won't lose suction it doesn't make it any better and you can't fool us. Minutes from the last AGM are available on request, but only after they have been lost, found, lost, found, lost and then found again at the bottom of the fruit bowl under the small brown furry thing that may once have been a plum but then again could equally be one of those baby koalas for the tops of pencils. Who's to tell?

The Non-Domestic Goddess Club of Great Britain expects its members to uphold extremely low standards at all times. Anyone nearly up-to-date with the ironing will have to explain themselves in full, while anyone totally up-to-date will be automatically expelled. Anyone who hasn't touched an iron in years and just tries to pass everything off as 100 per cent linen (including their face) will be awarded free life membership. Ditto anyone who makes Nescafé by placing the mug under the hot tap, both when pressed for time and when not, and who prepares bedding between guests by turning the pillow over to its 'fresh' side. The Non-Domestic Goddess Club has this to say about blackened cookware: soak, soak, soak, then throw away when nobody is looking. The Club also suggests never questioning the fact that there is an *A to Z* in your underwear drawer, as well as a toy knight, some small change (amounting to 87p), a book on houseplants and three Fox's Glacier Fruits. To question can only lead to madness. The Non-Domestic Goddess Club of Great Britain has this to say about socks with holes in: put aside for darning, then throw away when nobody is looking.

The Non-Domestic Goddess Club suggests never,

ever going right to the bottom of the laundry basket, as anything could be living down there. The Club fully endorses opening the top of the laundry basket, sighing dispiritedly and promptly closing it again. The Club expects all members to have all of the following items at the back of at least one kitchen cupboard: a tin of golden syrup with the lid half-cocked (treacle is also acceptable); an ancient pot of hundreds and thousands; a spilling bag of decade-old lentils; several bottles of food colouring (all green); a variety of exotic pickles and chutneys which seemed like a good idea at the time; any number of herbal teas with tempting names like Mango Carnival and Tropical Fiesta which no one drinks because they all taste of pond; sticky jars of stuff that can no longer be identified and have bits of old moth wing, spilled lentils and fairy-cake cases stuck to their sides. The Club has this to say about leftovers: decant carefully into Tupperware, place in fridge, leave for a week, then throw out when nobody is looking.

Alternatively, place in freezer, leave for a decade, then throw out when nobody is looking. Never throw anything away today that you can keep and then throw away at a later date.

The Non-Domestic Goddess Club of Great Britain does not advise leaving washing in the washing machine until it smells, as this will only mean having to do it again, but accepts that such things can happen. We also strongly advise never serving food within its sell-by date as the sudden absence of harmful bacteria may lead to diarrhoea and vomiting. Should food drop on the floor, it is extremely important to blow on it a bit before putting it back on the plate, preferably when nobody is looking. It is perfectly acceptable to start something and then not finish it, unless it is a bottle of gin. The Club has sympathy for anyone who has tried to defrost a chicken in the bath or dry a child's swimming costume, just unpacked from last week's lesson, by swinging it round her head. The Club has this to say to anyone who is about 19 years behind with the ironing: gather it all up and throw it away while nobody is looking. Alternatively, bury it at the bottom of the garden, along with the pet goldfish whose bowl was used as an ashtray but died of natural causes all the same.

We hope you have enjoyed this short introduction to the Non-Domestic Goddess Club of Great Britain and that you will always defend the useless housewife whatever. Some people say that the trouble with useless housewives is that they are lazy and just sit around all day reading *Hello!*, whereas, in truth, they work really, really hard. It's just that so much of what they do happens when nobody is looking.

The Non-Domestic Goddess Club Newsletter

(As Written on the Back of a Cheque Book)

'Firstly, if not solely, as we rarely achieve much, we would like to thank Mrs Wentworth who, still in her pyjama bottoms at 3 p.m., and with hair that looked as if it had been done with an electric toothbrush — a look we fully endorse, by the way — came in to give us a talk entitled 'The Last Taboo'. We all got very excited, even Mrs Agnew, who for years has been answering her phone with, 'Hello, Drudge Central. Main drudge here,' and might be quite badly depressed. She once didn't get out of bed for several weeks even though her husband tried to tempt her downstairs with a new apron and a fresh bottle of Flash and promised not to mention the ironing buried at the bottom of the garden ever again.

Everyone chatted about what Mrs Wentworth might mean but none of us got anywhere near. 'Right, here goes,' said Mrs Wentworth, after hitching up her pyjama bottoms in a very professional way and then taking the podium. 'I am about to break a taboo. I'm going to dare speak its name and that name is . . . greaseproof paper.' Well, at that, Susie Banks gave a little shriek while Jenny Marks fair fainted. 'Yes,' continued Mrs Wentworth, 'greaseproof paper. There, I have said it again.' There were gasps all round. 'We all know about clingfilm,' she proceeded, 'and how malevolent that can be.' We all nodded. 'We all know how it sticks to everything but that which you want it to stick to. We all further know that, most particularly, it will stick so spitefully to itself that you have to scrunch that sheet into a tight ball and toss it in the bin so you can start with a fresh sheet that will stick to itself and have to be thrown in the bin, too. This can go right on to the end of the roll which, ladies, does make you think: all things considered, what is the point of clingfilm, beyond a great deal of scrunching and bad-temperedness?' 'Hear, hear,' we all chorused. 'And we all know about tin foil, too,' she added. 'How, if you get a little nick in it, it'll come off in little slivers that are no use at all. We know about that.' 'Hear, hear,' we all chorused again.

'But greaseproof paper? Ladies, why are we never warned about greaseproof paper? Why, in particular, don't women tell other women about greaseproof paper? Sisters, what is going on here?' We all looked a little sheepish at that. 'Is it some kind of female conspiracy?' asked Mrs Wentworth. 'Like that surrounding childbirth, and the unspoken rule that no woman should ever tell another woman what it is truly like? Is that it? And so we are left to discover the full horror for ourselves?'

We thought this was probably the case. We agreed that if you ask a woman what childbirth is truly like she will possibly say something along the lines of, 'It's a little bit painful,' whereas what she actually means is: 'OK, imagine someone has stuffed a vast shipment of hand grenades up your uterus, timed to go off at increasingly frequent intervals with increasing violence over a 17-hour period but, hey, it's all worth it at the end when they hand you a little baby – your little baby! – and you think: "Hell's bells, what have I done? I can't love this. I don't even know how it works. Put it in a home! Give it to a nice couple who can't have children of their own!"' Jenny Marks said this is how it always happens because if women were to actually spell out how bad it is there is no way other women would ever have babies. 'Perhaps, similarly,' suggested Mrs Wentworth, 'if women told other women how evil greaseproof paper is no one would ever make cakes, and everybody loves cake.' We could

10

not fault her logic there. We do all love cakes. But what she said next took us rather by surprise.

'Have you ever,' she asked, 'tried to make a three-layer cake?' We said we had not. We said, further, that we felt Mrs Wentworth had let the Club down by even attempting such a thing. 'Well, it was for a child's birthday,' she said, as if that was any excuse. We said our own children prefer shop-bought cakes. Mrs Agnew even said that she once spent all night making a cake for her son who, when he saw it, burst into tears and said, 'But I wanted a Power Ranger one from Tesco!' The cake was, she admitted, flat and lopsided and she'd forgotten to put the sugar in, but what do you expect from someone so badly depressed?

Mrs Wentworth continued: 'If you have attempted a three-layer cake, the first instruction will probably tell you to cut out three discs from a roll of – and I'm going to say it again here, ladies – greaseproof paper. So you cut out the first disc. Hey, you are beginning to think, this isn't that hard. You then cut out the second disc. Nothing to it. But then, just as you are going for the third, you will note that the first disc has spontaneously leapt and curled itself into the shape of a fat cigar.' 'Yes, yes,' we all cried. 'That's exactly what happens!' 'And while you are noting that the first disc has leapt and curled itself into the shape of a fat cigar — and are thinking, "Well, there's a thing" — the second disc will not only curl up likewise, but will skip brazenly along the worktop as it does so.' 'Yes, yes,' we all cried. 'That's exactly what happens. The bloody nerve of it.' 'And then,' said Mrs Wentworth, 'you are forced to chase it, catch it and smooth it back out. You smooth out the first disc, too, but as you are doing so, what happens? The second disc not only curls up again but actually jumps off the worktop. You retrieve it and smooth it back out. It jumps and curls again. So does the first disc.

'You will try everything to keep the discs flat. I can see, ladies, that you know what I mean. You will try with your fingers, palms, elbows, entire forearms, your arse. No joy. You will think: "I know, I will spread butter on to the baking tray and press them down on to that." No joy. And do you know why? Because greaseproof paper is, it turns out, grease proof. How sly is that? In the end you will have to weigh down the perimeters with stones from the garden but by that time you've had it, really. You'll tell the child you'll be getting a cake from Tesco. The child will try to look as if he or she isn't deeply, deeply disappointed, may even holler "Yippee", but we know. A mother can always tell.'

Mrs Wentworth concluded on a strong note. 'I do hope that, now the whole issue is out in the open, women will be able to talk more freely about greaseproof paper abuse, whether it is happening to them now, has happened to them in the past, or whether they have even had a disc curl up, jump, poke them in the eye and then shoot through the cat-flap. I also hope that, from now on, you will all think twice about keeping your clingfilm and greaseproof paper in the same kitchen drawer: they are only egging each other on in there.'

We thanked Mrs Wentworth very much for her interesting talk which, on the whole, we preferred to Jenny Marks's talk on how best to rotate dusters, which would have been inexcusable if she hadn't been almost too drunk to stand up. Next week, a group discussion on the Fine Art of Resentful Cooking, which everybody does but nobody talks about either.

The Fine Art of Resentful Cooking

The NDGC (GB) accepts its members will probably have to cook for the family on numerous occasions, but that's fine. Home cooking, as Nigella Lawson has so often pointed out, is not about getting fancy recipes absolutely right. It's about love, warmth, sitting together around the table and talking about the day, or would be except in those instances when you're just not up to it, which may be quite often. As such, we would like to direct you to *The Resentful Kitchen*,* the cookbook and NDGC publication which remains the definitive work on how to go about it bitterly while bashing pans around in an exceedingly grudging and furious manner. The following recipe for omelette and salad is perfect for those times when

---

* *The Resentful Kitchen* is available from most good bookshops and all bad-tempered ones.

it's late, you've just got in, the last thing you want to
do is prepare a meal, but there they all are, looking
up at you open-mouthed and expectantly, as if you
might have perfectly chargrilled little fillet steaks
down your socks and a heavenly meringue confection
in your bra. 'Here it is, guys! Come and get it.
Thanks for waiting!'

Ingredients:

Eggs; lettuce; a cucumber, sliced, but only if you feel
you can use a knife without stabbing someone
through the heart with it.

Method:

First, set face to somewhere between cross and really,
really cross. Prepare salad by shredding lettuce. This
can often be done just by looking at it. If using
cucumber, and wishing to avoid sharp knife owing to
homicidal urges, rip it apart with your bare hands or
use the nearest blunt instrument, like your husband's
head. Crack eggs on teeth, which should now be
nicely bared, then beat eggs with a phenomenal
amount of anger and spite and maybe some spit will
accidentally get into the mixture. Who's to know,
especially if you do it when nobody is looking?
Incinerate the lot in a frying pan while hurling
insults. Serve in front of telly as the last thing you

want to hear about is their day, which is never that interesting anyway.

Serving Suggestions:

Good accompaniments include your own body weight in alcohol and an icy and contemptuous: 'Happy now?' If not sufficiently icy, put back in freezer and check in an hour.

But We Love Nigella!

We all love Nigella, it's true. What is there not to love? She's an icon. But if you feel, as many of our Club members do, that she has been somewhat mistreated by Channel 4, then do sign this letter and forward it to the station. She deserves no less.

An Open Letter to Channel 4

To whom it may concern,

I am writing this to say that I believe Ms Nigella Lawson has, over the years, been most cruelly ill served by Channel 4 and to ask if you have any plans to rectify the situation. To get straight to the point, Ms Lawson is obviously a most sloppy eater — my two-year-old is significantly cleaner at the table — and such are the lax production standards at your company that you have never made any attempt to disguise this unsavoury and, if I may say so, off-putting fact. On occasion, I have not only seen Ms Lawson with steaming juices dribbling down her chin but have I also witnessed her digging her fingers into various dishes and then licking them with such mouth-filled sighs of delight that, for all the world, you'd think she was performing some kind of sexual act. I'm sure this is not what you intended.

I'm writing in the hope you will do something to save Ms Lawson from any further embarrassment. As it is, whenever my partner and I have watched any of Nigella's programmes, he in particular has been so appalled and disgusted by her messy and unhygienic eating habits that he has had to move nearer the television, just to check that what he is seeing is actually true. Sometimes, the whole business affects his stomach so badly that he has had to put a hand down the waistband of his trousers and rub to achieve any kind of symptomatic relief. There have even been instances where, traumatised as he is and unable to expel such appalling images from his mind, he has even called out her name while we have been having sex. He has never called out Delia's name, which, I believe, must be taken as a tribute to the BBC's infinitely superior professionalism and hygiene standards. Please take this on board.

Don't get me wrong. I love Nigella, just as I love

her Living Kitchen range. I even own one of her ceramic storage jars (duck-egg blue) in an amphora form that can be used in either an upright or tilted position and comes with a glass lid that allows at-a-glance identification of contents. I keep my biscuits in it and would not now wish to live without it. My previous jar did not come with a glass lid allowing at-a-glance identification of contents so I had to remember what biscuits were in it, and sometimes I got this wrong. I am sure you'll agree that there is nothing to match the disappointment of thinking you are about to get a Jaffa Cake but pulling out a Rich Tea instead. Ms Lawson's jar represents a great advance when it comes to jars of this kind. I like mine tilted. Please pass on my regards when next you speak to her but, more importantly, please review your production standards so that Ms Lawson can reclaim some dignity. I'm sure she'd just die if she knew she looked as if she was doing something sexual every time she licked a bowl!

Yours etc.,

....

(Your signature should be followed by 'Member of the Non-Domestic Goddess Club of Great Britain'. Your letter will go nowhere near the top, which will be all dusty anyway.)

The All-Important Lifestyle Question

Aside from anything else you must, these days, have what is called 'a lifestyle'. But where can you get one if you suspect you are without? Well, having asked around, the Club has learned that the Conran Shop do good lifestyles — pricey, but worth it, by all accounts — whereas the Argos lifestyles (Catalogue Number: 678/234) are good value but quite bottom-of-the-range. (Forget Ikea. Ikea will only do your head in. So many veneers, so little time . . .) John Lewis's lifestyles are, of course, never knowingly undersold, which is reassuring, but they do not keep them in stock. You have to order and await delivery, which can be a problem if it arrives when you are not in. This either means having to go to a Royal Mail collection point on a desolate industrial estate at a time that is almost deliriously inconvenient (4 a.m.–4.15 a.m., say) or it

will be delivered to a neighbour, who may open it, decide it is the lifestyle they've always wanted, and then refuse to give it back. This can be extremely infuriating.

Indeed, can there be anything more infuriating than sharing a street with someone who is living the lifestyle that is rightfully yours? There cannot. As one Club member recently told us: 'I have long suspected that my neighbour, Sue, stole my lifestyle at some point. It is certainly the lifestyle I ordered, with its solid oak floors, breathtaking kitchen extension, pedigree Schnauzer, forensic surfaces, fresh lilies in the hall, and even remote controls with all the backs of the battery compartments still intact. Sue denies that it is my lifestyle. "You may want it to be your lifestyle," she says, "and you may envy me having this lifestyle, but it is my lifestyle and it always has been." Obviously, I now no longer talk to Sue and kick her dog when I can. The thing that they never tell you about lifestyles is that not only can they come between people, but dogs may get dented.'

Of course, you can try Comet for a lifestyle, but we would not advise it (see Cometitis, below). Aside from anything else, Comet will almost certainly try to sell you an expensive but entirely useless extended warranty should your lifestyle leak, explode or prove faulty in the next five years. Steer clear. The manufacturer's own guarantee should cover a new lifestyle, at least for the first few years, anyway. Never buy a lifestyle on credit without first closely checking the APR and the feng shui clause. Should there be such a clause, insist it is struck out. You have, according to the National Consumer Council, every right to do so. Say you accept that feng shui is an ancient and venerated art but you are perfectly capable of putting things where you are least likely to fall over them yourself, thanks very much. Be very clear about exactly what you do want. Say something like: 'I want what Sue's got but only if I can drive it home myself.'

Should you manage to acquire a lifestyle, you must tend to it. It would be great if lifestyles looked after themselves, ticking over nicely all the while, but they simply don't. This is why you must find someone trustworthy and qualified to 'guru' it. This is what a lifestyle guru does. Carole Caplin is often described as a 'lifestyle guru' and it's actually quite frightening to think that if it were not for 'lifestyle gurus' there would be no point to Carole Caplin whatsoever. Absolutely none at all. A word of warning, though: there are a lot of cowboy lifestyle gurus around, as recently exposed on *Watchdog*. Remember the guru who was secretly filmed charging £200 per hour —

£200 an hour! – but who spent most of that time out in the van 'getting an essential part, without which your lifestyle simply will not work, love'? Yeah, right. These people have no morals and will even diddle pensioners. 'Just passing, love, and I couldn't help noticing a bit of your lifestyle has come loose . . .'

Anyway, here are some tips for choosing a lifestyle guru, as recommended by *Which?*

1) If you get a phone call or a knock on the door from someone 'doing lifestyle guru work in your area', don't even think about it unless you can talk to and see the work already completed for a satisfied customer.

2) Make sure that the guru has premises, rather than simply a mobile number. If, for example, your lifestyle starts making banging sounds in the middle of the night or steadfastly refuses to go to Pilates, you will need to know you can get hold of your guru whatever.

3) You are asking for trouble if you make a deal over the doorstep or in your living room. Inevitably you will be subjected to a very hard sell from a very skilful and sometimes unscrupulous salesperson, highly motivated by commission, who will point to the batteries as they roll under

the settee and say, 'Do you really want to live like this?' 'No,' you will say, bursting into tears. And there they will have you.

Oh Dear, Cometitis

You may, of course, choose to ignore the warning about Comet, but that would be dumb. The trouble with Comet is that, after any dealings with them, it is possible to catch Cometitis, an extremely unpleasant illness. The following is a Club member's first-person account of what it is like to have the disease and you must take it as a warning of the gravest kind:

I am sorry if this is all a ramble and don't make the much sense and this writing gone all to pot but it is because I am in the bed and am very sick with the Cometitis which you catch when you goes to the Comet and buys something and it all goes wrong, and you find you are trapped in the dark underworld that is laffingly called Comet After-Sales Service, ha, ha! (That is mad laff, by the way, of someone not quite right in the head, because of the Cometitis.)

I did call the doctor who has just bin, and he
say I have this Cometitis real bad, and that he knows
of people who have died of this illness because the
will to live just seeps away and I should try to get
up if I can. But I do not think I can, because the
thing about Cometitis is that it comes with big
murderous feelings and I know that if I was to get
up I would go to the Comet with a machine-gun and
mow them all down while refusing to give my
surname or direct line because it is company policy
that the customer person should never be able to
speak to the same person twice. And they say this is
Comet Sense. Ha ha! That is the mad hollow laff
again, which is so characteristic of this very bad
sickness.

The worst thing is I knows I bought this illness on
to myself, and that if I had gone to the John Lewis in
the first place I would not be suffering like I am now.
But I needed an oven and I needed one quick because
ours went kaput and I thought I would go to the
Comet instead of the John Lewis because at the
Comet they have the ovens in stock and I did not want
to wait for the delivery. So I goes to the Comet and
says I would like a single electric oven, and so the man
called Rizwan says, 'Here are our ovens,' and I asks,
'Why is this oven more expensive than that oven?' and
he says he don't know and yawns and so I say, 'I'll have

that oven, thank you', and he says it is not in stock
and neither is that one nor that one and so I takes the
Zanussi ZBF260 White (£225) because that is in
stock, and I do not think Rizwan will be able to keep
awake for much longer. But then, when I gets to
paying, he gets all the lively and says he can offer me
an extended warranty for just the £80. But I say I do
not want a warranty, thank you, so he says he will do it
for just the £50, and I say no thank you and he say,
'Madam, I tell you what, I will make the oven £175,
and give you a £50 warranty and that ways you still
spends the same.' And I says OK, and so I gets this
warranty which means that if the oven breaks down in
six years, for examps, I can wait in for three weeks for
someone to come see it and then they can tell me that
it is not worth the fixing.

And so I leaves with the oven that the Rizwan say I
can just plug in when I gets home. But when I gets
home and gets the oven out the bubbledy wrap I find
there is no plug at the back and no cable neither. So I
calls the Comet people and press the 1 and the 2 and
listens to how important my call is, which is why no
one is answering and then 79 hours later I talks to the
Natalie who says I must have it fitted by qualified
lectrician and one will come a week on Friday, by
which time the John Lewis could have delivered 49
times. But I think I will stick with it having got this

far, which is always a mistake because it is bound to lead to full-blown Cometitis.

And so I waits in on Friday but nobody comes, so I phone back the Comet and presses the 1 and the 2 then they says no one has a record of this booking and they never heard of this Natalie and now someone will come a week on Tuesday, and on Tuesday nobody comes so I phone back the Comet and presses the 1 and the 2 and 89 hours later I speaks to Sheila who says she has no record of the booking and someone will come a week on Wednesday and she doesn't think it is necessary to put out a missin persons bulletin for Natalie, no. And a week on Wednesday a man *does* come and he say sorry he do not come a week ago last Tuesday but he was sick, which is odd thing to say as there was no record of booking, but then he do fit the oven and he do say, 'All done, love.' And then after he go I do put the oven on to make a nice dinner because a nice dinner would be nice after a monf with no oven, but when I switches the oven on it goes BANG and all the lectric in the house goes off. BANG!

And so I phones the Comet again (0870 542 5425), who now say this is a problem for the service engineers (01992 702 470), who say this is a problem for the customer services (0870 542 5425), who say this is a problem for the service engineers (01992

702 470), who say . . . And so I say, 'I have got no
lights, no heat, no phones, and the fridge it already
be dripping! I am calling you on the spensive mobile
by torchlight.' And so the Sharon on the other end
says she will send a qualified lectrician in a week to fix
it and I says, 'A week?' and then I starts to cry. And
Sharon thinks about a new place to pass this thing
called the buck and says this is really a problem for
the store (020-8361 8056) and so I phones the store
and Pramit says he will call back within the hour but
he does not. And so I goes to bed with the Cometitis
and the murderous feelings and lots of pairs of
socks on.

Then I wakes in the morning and think, no, I will
not surrender to this bad thing called Cometitis, so I
gets up, puts on all the clothes I have, eats everything
in the fridge cos it do be going off, rings the Comet
press office and speaks to this man Andy Richardson
(a surname!). So I says to this Mr Richardson who I
calls 'Mr Richardson' because it is so thrillin to have a
surname that I am from the papers and am doing a
story about Comet customers being left with no
lectric and he agrees that is bad and 20 minutes later
a man come and he done fix it. So what I am saying to
you is that if you get the Cometitis do not call 0870
542 5425 or 01992 702 470 or 020-8361 8056.
Just call the press office – 01923 710000 – and say

you is from the papers because they don't know no different. You might even say you are from the *Which?* if you really wants to put the wind up them. And now I am going backs to bed because it takes a long time to get over the Cometitis, but if you gets it at least you now know what to do and who to call, ha, ha. That is still mad laff of someone not quite right in the head but the doctor do say he is hopeful of a full recovery so longs as I never go back to Comet — ever — and usually I lies to my doctor and tell him I don't smoke when I do but this time I tells him I will do as he says. And I will.

Vinegar, the Answer to Everything?

Yes. Totally. Which is why we are so pleased to announce the introduction of a new, unique, NDGC advice service — the Vinegar Clinic — whereby you may ask anything and the answer will always be the same: vinegar. This is because vinegar *is* the answer to everything. Kim and Aggie from *How Clean is Your House?* are always going on about it. Advice columns are always going on about it. What's the best way to clean limescale from my kettle? Vinegar. How can I clean my dusty dried-flower arrangement? Vinegar. How can I get water marks off wood? Vinegar. The service has received many queries already, which include:

Dear Vinegar Clinic
  I feel lost and confused in the world, and wonder if you might be good enough to inform me of the meaning of life?
Vinegar.

Dear Vinegar Clinic

    I'm a big fan of Elkie Brooks and would like to know, was she ever in a band and, if so, what was it called?

Vinegar . . . something. We forget now.

Dear Vinegar Clinic

    I've been invited to a party tonight but am nervous about going as I'm very, very shy. Can you suggest ways to boost my confidence?

One part vinegar mixed with 12 parts Bailey's and 72 parts Absolut should do it.

Dear Vinegar Clinic

    My husband is always turning the heating off, even though I feel the cold most keenly. Before I opt for killing him, is there something that I might splash in his eyes that would cause maximum stinging and discomfort.

Vinegar.

Dear Vinegar Clinic

    My birthday's coming up and I'd like a new scent but can't decide whether to ask for Chanel Number Five, Gucci Rush or Lovely by Sarah Jessica Parker. What do you think?

Have you considered vinegar?

Dear Vinegar Clinic

*I'm due to have my first baby — a girl — but my husband and I
simply cannot agree on a name. I favour Old Testament names
(Rachel, Rebecca) whereas he is more into the New Testament
(Susannah, Carmel). Can you think of a suitable compromise?*
Vinegar.

Dear Vinegar Clinic

*My family and I love chips and eat them nightly. However, I'm
always looking for new ways to serve them. Could you suggest a
condiment that would best bring out the flavour? We have already
tried salt, tomato ketchup, mayonnaise and salad cream, but are
looking for something maltier, more liquid, and maybe deep brown in
colour. Any ideas?*
Nope, sorry. You've got us stumped there.

If you have questions, you may write to this service at
the Vinegar Clinic, Vinegar House, Vinegar Street,
Vinegarsville, Malt Lake City, Utah. Alternatively,
just put 'Freepost Vinegar' on the envelope. It won't
get there either but at least you haven't wasted money
on a stamp.

A Last Word from the Non-Domestic Goddess Club

The Club expects extremely low standards to be upheld in the garden as well as the house. Most importantly, it expects its members to buy lots of packets of seeds and then keep them for ever and ever in a kitchen drawer, along with the dead batteries, old guarantees and scraps of leftover wrapping paper. The Club is happy to embrace anyone who has given up gardening altogether. The Club has this to say about gardening generally: any plants you wish to thrive will die and those you wish to die will thrive. The Club realises this: a garden will enslave you and eat up all your cash while allowing you to think it is somehow free and liberating. Members must also purchase lots of bulbs which they will never plant, hide for years, then throw away when nobody is looking.

2

Children:
The Real,
Real Facts

*H*aving a child is the most important thing you will
ever do and, as the childcare experts say, loving it
'is the best investment there is.' However, we would
add this only applies if you do not count property. A
two-bedroom flat in St John's Wood purchased in
1990, for example, will be worth much more today
than a child born in the same year. Also, that two-
bedroom flat in St John's Wood is not now a teenager
leaving wet towels all over his bedroom floor (although
returning it to the bathroom would involve what? A
walk of three yards?) So you could say, then, that
property is the best investment there is, and loving a
child isn't much of an investment at all (a walk of three
yards, yet it would save so much resentment!) but if we
all bought property and didn't have children, one day
we would run out of people to live in those properties.
This is why it is important to have children and why so

many of us do. This is also why you cannot trust child-care experts, whose advice shifts hourly as it is: dummies are fine; dummies are not fine; take baby into bed with you; don't take baby into bed with you; put baby to sleep on its back; put baby to sleep on its front; put baby to sleep balanced on its nose – delicately, now – with its feet pointing towards Pluto, no Jupiter, no Pluto, no Jupiter. Is it any wonder that most parents, at some point, think, 'I wish I'd bought that two-bed flat in St John's Wood'? However, here we offer you the top ten absolutely certain facts – and no mistake – about children:

1) The more effort you put into a child's packed lunch – especially if it has meant a midnight trip to the all-night garage for supplies – the less chance it will be eaten.
2) A teenage girl will not be fully happy with her attire unless she has caught you wincing. (Gasping is better, but wincing will do.)
3) A child shown one of your old, treasured Ladybird books will always say, 'What, they go and get their feet measured in a shoe shop and that's the story, that's it?'*

*Note: They don't even like the one with the bus. 'What, they get to go on a bus and that's it, that's the story?'

4) The school play will always have one child who knows all the lines shouting into the faces of those who don't. (And they call this quality entertainment?)

5) No boy will ever say, 'But, Mum, I don't want you wasting your hard-earned money on those expensive football boots. The cheaper ones will do.'

6) No child has ever resented its mother for stealing his or her birthday money to pay the milkman, and anyway it's the elves that do it.

7) The more you press an outer garment on a child the more he or she will resist.

8) A child's interest in tractors and dinosaurs will persist long after your interest has waned, assuming you had any interest in the first place, which is unlikely.

9) Swimming goggles will always leak or be too tight and it will somehow always be your fault.

10) A child's school bag will always contain, along with the rotting organic matter of unknown origin, four out-of-date letters saying how important it is that you come to the meeting that was two months ago as well as a note saying a child in the class has nits and we're not saying it's your child exactly, but do you get our drift?

Younger Children, Their Care, and a Good Ludo Tip

As is well known, and has been documented in literature many times, younger children are small and can need quite a lot of care. Many people find this annoying. They also frequently demand to be played with, which many people find annoying, too. However, as our members agree, one excellent tip is to hide increasing amounts of your money under the board during Monopoly, which almost guarantees you'll be out in no time. 'Oh, look. Can you credit it? I'm bust already.' When it comes to Ludo or Snakes & Ladders there may be no alternative but to swallow the dice. As a general rule of thumb, it is always wise to play to lose, because then it is all over so much quicker. The winner may take all, but the loser always makes the fastest exit. You may want to play table tennis with your eyes shut.

Alternatively, don't be afraid to ask other people, like grandparents, to muck in. Although it will break your heart, you may wish to leave the children with their grandparents all day. You may even dispatch them with a small overnight bag, just in case you are hard pressed to pick them up any time in the near future. Grandparents may protest and say, 'Helping out is one thing', or 'This is ridiculous', or 'Can't it wait until your father is out of intensive care?' or 'We are too old to be running after little ones', but they are just being silly. For a start, there are lots of things you can do with children sitting down, like kayaking. Do see the children in, if you want, but sometimes it just makes sense to put them on the doorstep, ring the bell and run. 'Surprise, Grandma!'

Alternatively, there are always childminders, and a good childminder is worth her weight in gold. Get a list of registered childminders from your local

council and when you meet each one ask yourself the
following questions: Is she friendly and accessible? Is
the environment safe? Are the children in her care
encouraged to play? Would she be happy to have the
kids for several months at a time? Should the first
childminder on the list turn out to be a chain smoker
with a Dobermann and a condemned electric fire in
her 29th-floor flat with no fire escape, do not dismiss
her there and then, especially if she is available to
start that very afternoon. It is easy to be prejudiced
against such people, particularly if, for example, she
leaves her flick knives and matches and crack
paraphernalia lying about. After all, she may be a
lovely person under all those piercings and tattoos.

Another option, of course, is a nanny. However,
ever since the whole Jude/nanny/Sienna business, the
general thinking among mothers is that a plain nanny
without a jot of sexual allure is quite the best kind.
A plain one with no sexual allure, halitosis, hairy legs
and disturbing personal habits is an even better kind.
However, check and double check her CV. She may say
she can burp the Westminster chimes, do armpit farts
and doesn't believe in deodorant but unless you talk to
her previous employers, how can you be really sure?
If she also has stiff little hairs on her chin, possibly
sprouting from a wart, chances are she'll be quite
pricey. In fact, a nanny like that can more or less write

her own ticket. If this is the option for you, try Really
Plain Nannies (www.reallyplainnannies.co.uk),
where you will also find many testimonials from
satisfied clients: 'Magda smells, eats us out of house
and home, runs up staggering phone bills, and tells
the children that if they don't eat lots of junk food
their heads will explode. My husband said it was him
or her. I chose her, so he has left us for good. No
chance of him sleeping with her now! Well done you,
for such a brilliant service!' Aupairs are fine, so long
as you don't mind them crying a lot and drinking all
the Tropicana even though they come from such poor
little war-torn countries you'd think they'd be grateful
for unpolluted tap water.

You could, of course, look after your children
yourself, but do think about this: how is it going to
make their grandparents feel?

The Primary School Summer Fair: A New Way Forward

The school summer fair is always the biggest event in the school calendar (if you do not, of course, count that other highlight: the non-competitive sports day where every child gets a ribbon, no matter how useless they are). The fair inevitably means that in the preceding weeks you will be button-holed by other parents asking how many hours you are willing to put in behind the plant stall ('Um . . . none?') or whether you want the early or the late face-painting shift ('How does "neither" sound?'). Then there is the fund-raising auction, whereby parents and staff sell their own particular skills. These auctions rarely offer the following lots, but wouldn't it be nice:

Lot # 1: Contract Killing

Mrs Walsh, our popular Reception teacher — her 'Knick Knack Paddy Whack', accompanied by guitar, is now available on cassette and CD — has again offered to take out a person of your choice. It could be a business competitor, a love rival, the plumber who doesn't turn up or one of those cocky estate agents in a customised Mini Cooper that we've all fantasised about gunning down. Mrs Walsh would like to make it very clear that the contract cannot be

exchanged for a homemade cake or cookies, as she is not at all keen on baking.

Lot # 2: Home Theatre

Cynthia and Douglas Askwith (parents of Ralph, pronounced 'Rafe', Year 4) will put on *A Chorus Line*, playing all the roles themselves, in your own front room or any other venue. Cynthia and Douglas are talented amateur thespians who will perform anywhere, given half a chance. And they are already busy rehearsing, performing 'One Singular Sensation' with canes and spangles at the school gate at picking-up time most afternoons. The school would like to take this opportunity not only to thank all other parents for giving Cynthia and Douglas space by sprinting off in the opposite direction, but also to say that Ralph (pronounced 'Rafe') is not a certainty for the title role in *Joseph*, even though Cynthia and Douglas have been sending him to school with a tea-towel on his head and a dead goat under his arm for some months now.

Lot # 3: Computer Tuition

One for the boys! Mr Leigh (head of IT) will come to your home and talk you through the best way of viewing hardcore porn on the internet without leaving a trail. Mr Leigh knows all the best sites, including 'Get Down on All Fours, Bitch!', 'Slag-Fest' and 'Slapper Up!', which can be hard to access discreetly if you don't have the proper know-how. If the children or their mother should interrupt, Mr Leigh will instantly pretend to be giving tips on how to get the best out of Ocado or how to bid for designer sunglasses on eBay. Mr Leigh will provide his own transport and change of trousers but may need snacks.

Lot # 4: Tuscan Holiday

Many, many thanks to Lucy and Benedict Caesar for their generosity in offering a week at their house in Tuscany yet again. However, although Lucy and Benedict are Old Labour through and through — always have been; always will be — they feel they must insist that the bidding starts at £10,000 to exclude the poorer elements in the school, who have nearly all been squeezed out now but we are not quite there yet. Still, only seven free school meal-takers to go! Flights are not included but the house does come with full-time liveried servants, who are also socialists, and a tennis court.

Lot # 5: Personal Slave

Our very own headmistress, Mrs Ball, has kindly offered to be your personal slave for the afternoon!

She'll weed, make tea, do the Hoovering and, should you wish, will even beat you like the naughty, naughty little boy you are. It is anticipated that this is going to be a highly sought-after lot — our dads seem to love it! — so do get your bids in early. Should you not wish to be beaten like the naughty, naughty little boy you are, Mrs Ball will do a small amount of ironing instead (pillowcases; sheets; T-shirts; no pleats, please!).

Lot # 6: Inside Information

Want to know which children have nits? Which are on the at-risk register? Which are allowed Sunny Delight? Which are simply out-and-out losers who will never amount to anything? Yes, help your own children pick the right sort of friends by bidding for this one-to-one session with Miss Saunders, our school nurse and welfare officer. Miss Saunders will use slides, as well as confidential medical and social services records, to help you identify those kids you'd rather your own didn't mix with. Never be caught out again encouraging a friendship only to find that the other child doesn't have any private music lessons or tutoring or even their own bedroom with books in it! Avoid those distressing, tearful scenes when you have to tell your child not to speak to that child ever again! First year offered, but bound to be popular.

Those Pesky Questions Younger Children Ask

(The NDGC knows that young children ask a lot of pesky questions. Here's our guide to answering them in a way that may not be entirely satisfactory but will get them off your back.)

Q: *Mummy, who is God?*

A: A big man in command of everything, particularly the remote control and use of the car, who lives in this house and is otherwise known as Daddy.

Q: *Mummy, can God see everything?*

A: I thought not until, noting that his eyes were closed and a 'Zzzz' sound that could not be blamed on a bee was filling the room, I tried to switch from Eurosport to *ER*. 'I saw that,' he said. 'Switch back.'

Q: *Mummy, is God omnipresent?*
A: Yes, particularly when there is only one glass of
   wine left in the bottle and you think he's
   otherwise occupied but as soon as you go for it,
   whoosh, there he is, getting in first and sometimes
   even rugby tackling you to the ground.

Q: *Mummy, are daddies necessary in this day and age?*
A: Yes, darling, on the whole, otherwise who would
   we laugh at when he spends most of a week
   assembling an Ikea bathroom cabinet upside
   down? You can't get that kind of amusement from
   someone anonymously ejaculating into a plastic
   jar for a fiver.

Q: *Mummy, is it true that some mummies make cakes and proper
   meals and do something called sewing?*
A: I've never heard such rot in my life. Who is filling
   your head with this misleading bile?

Q: *Mummy, what does Carole Caplin actually do?*
A: You've stumped me there, dear.

Q: *Mummy, what is dope?*
A: Dope is Daddy, darling, who assembles bathroom
   cabinets upside down and then insists it is meant
   to open from the top. I'm afraid, sweetie, that I

am just not ready to discuss his attempt to hang
the ready-made blind that promptly fell off.

Q: *Mummy, are you sure daddies are necessary in this day and age?*
A: I'm beginning to have second thoughts, I admit.

Q: *Mummy, what is sex?*
A: Something you occasionally have to do when there
is no Eurosport on telly and Daddy can't
reassemble the bathroom cabinet the right way up
because he has 'lost' the Allen key and he can't
rehang the blind because he has 'lost' the
hammer.

Q: *Mummy, what is an Allen key?*
A: It's what daddies say they have 'lost' when
mummies get at them for never doing DIY.

Q: *Mummy, is it ever all right to lie?*
A: Ask your father, and while you're at it, ask him
why Mummy recently discovered 79 Allen keys, 65
hammers, 27 radiator keys and a power drill
buried at the bottom of the garden.

Q: *Mummy, what is divorce?*
A: It's something you do to daddies when they
promise to change light bulbs but don't and you

end up standing on a chair and almost breaking your neck though he's tall enough to do it without a chair and no risk to life and limb, but can he be bothered?

Q: *Mummy — tell me — how many people does it take to change a light bulb in our house?*

A: One, because it's always me, isn't it?

Q: *Mummy, are you sure daddies are necessary in this day and age?*

A: Actually, no. Let's get a dog.

The Secondary School Boy, and Some Observations that are Very True

*H*ere is what the Club knows to be true about boys who have just started secondary school:

The boy will plead, constantly and without mercy, for a mobile phone, while the mother resists, not only because there is every chance he will be duffed up and 'jacked' by older boys on the bus, but because his telephone skills have yet to prove especially deserving. The phone will ring at home. 'It's for you,' the mother will say. The boy will pick up. 'Yeah, bye,' he will say. He will then hang up.

'Who was that?' the mother will ask.

'Freddie,' the boy will say.

'What did he want?'

'He wanted to know if I was busy this afternoon.'

The mother is reassured that, should she acquiesce

on the mobile front – as she will inevitably do as there is only so much a mother can take – the bill is guaranteed to be on the smallish side. The mother does not know, yet, that when he does get a mobile phone there is no guarantee he will ever answer it. In the unlikely instance he will return one of the mother's calls he will say, 'Mum, what do you want? This is costing me.' The mother may then say, 'Costing you? Costing you? OK, where to start? For brevity's sake – and because I respect you will have to pay for this out of your own money which happens to be the same money your father and I give you every month – let's skip babyhood and go straight to first shoes, then second shoes, third, fourth, fifth . . . and summer shoes and winter shoes and football boots for soft ground (studs) and football boots for hard ground (pimples) and cricket spikes and tennis trainers and trendy shoes which have to be replaced by trendier shoes because the initial shoes are no longer trendy because no one's into Etnies anymore, Mum, the skate look is just so over, where have you been . . .?' The mother may find that the line goes dead quite promptly.

The boy will lose everything. Already, he will be on his third locker key, fourth set of house keys and sixth lunch card. There is still, as far as the mother knows, an entire PE kit, seven jumpers, two coats and a tennis racket circling north London on the top deck of the W7. The loss of these items will not be the boy's fault because, as he will say, with an air of being wronged, 'It's not my fault.' When the mother has to go down the Tube station to get him his 35th London Transport photocard of the term, the nice woman in the office, whom mother now greets by name, laughs when she fills in the '2008' expiry date. The mother will laugh, too, but her laugh will be a hollow one.

The boy will come home from school, tie hanging out of pocket, shirt untucked, PE kit left on the bus, kick off a shoe, peel off a sock — better to get at whatever fungal infection he happens to have on the go — and sprawl on the sofa in the hope of an undisturbed tellyfest and toe-scratch until the middle of the following week. The mother, who knows better but simply cannot help herself, will annoy him a great deal by attacking him with foot powder while enquiring about his day. 'What did you do at school?' she will ask. 'Nuffin',' he will say. 'Any homework?' she will ask. 'Any homework?' she will repeat. 'Nah,' he will say, turning up the volume on the telly. The next morning, at 7.10 a.m., the boy will be spotted writing furiously in an exercise book. The mother will ask if this is the homework he doesn't have. He will say, 'Go away. It's just stuff.'

This will be the general pattern until, one evening, he will suddenly announce that the project on Nelson Mandela he was given a month ago is due in tomorrow. If the mother is a good mother she will know all there is to know about Nelson Mandela by 4 a.m. and will be hoping for an A. She will be pleased with her illustrations, painstakingly sourced on the internet and cut out with an impressively steady hand. If the mother is a bad mother, and a drinker, the Nelson Mandela project will make no sense whatsoever, be riddled with non-judicious spelling mistakes and the pictures will all be skew-whiff. The mother will get a D3 and will never be relied upon to do the boy's homework again. The mother may find it hard to feel heartbroken.

The boy will no longer consider girls as bad as they once were, even though the mother may be able to recall the country dancing episode at primary school when he pulled his jumper over his hands so he didn't actually have to touch a Lauren or a Robyn. The girls' shifting friendships with each other are now so extreme that the boy may well be likened to a big silly Labrador padding through a nest of vipers. The boy will now receive the occasional phone call from a girl. However, the boy's telephone manner being what it is, he will only be capable of barking one or both of the following:

'How did *you* get my number?' and: 'What do *you* want?'

Mother feels the contraception talk can wait, but is aware of dark mutterings about boys who are 'going out' with girls. 'Where do they go?' the mother will want to know. 'You don't go out when you're going out,' the boy will say. 'So how are we defining going out?' the mother will ask. If the boy thinks that obliging with a certain amount of information will help him in his mobile phone campaign, he will say, 'If a boy asks a girl out and she says "yes", then they are going out.'

'So they sort of hang out in school and stuff?'

'No.'

'I don't think I understand.'

'If a boy asks a girl out and she says "yes" they are going out, but then they're too embarrassed to speak to each other.'

'So, really, going out means avoiding one another?'

'Yeah, until one dumps the other, then they can be friends again.'

The mother is glad to get this sorted. The mother now appreciates that 'going out' is, in effect, a state of being.

The boy, who used to cling to his mother's leg and who worshipped her even when she didn't deserve it —

'Get off my leg, get off, get off!' – now acts as if she is a boring old drag, not worth tuppence. The mother knows this is nonsense. The mother knows that while her parents were middle aged and boring and a drag when she was young, she is not. The mother may even say, 'It's not true that I live in John Lewis. Sometimes I don't go for a whole morning!' The mother knows she is hip, hip, hip. The mother may think that the boy needs to wake up and smell the coffee, which has to be better than Lynx (Africa), a masculine fragrance that would be delightful if it didn't make her gag so.

The boy will now have transferred all his affection to his father. He will do this without a backward glance, even though the mother has, over the years, proved herself an accomplished bottom-wiper, Father Christmas, party-organiser, nit-picker, foot-powderer, laundress, chauffeur, cook and expert lost-property forager. This will now count for nothing. The boy will see the mother only as a dental appointment Nazi and bedtime fascist. The father, who has never nit-picked, foot-powdered or party-organised, but is lax about dental hygiene and does let the boy fall asleep in front of soft porn on Channel 5, will now be seen as God.

The mother will find this hurtful until she realises that, as the boy no longer cares about her, she no longer has to care about his sporting fixtures. The mother realises she is thus freed from watching football on freezing Sunday mornings and shouting 'good tackle' at random intervals just to appear interested. The mother realises there is a lot to be said for now being the Parent Who Does Not Matter. The mother has even been known to shout 'Yippee' as they go out the door on a Sunday morning.

So this is what is known about boys who have just started secondary school, and who will inevitably leave something on the bus today. Most mothers hope it's the fungal infection.

At last, the Teenopedia!

*H*ere, at long last, all the facts and figures you will ever need to know about teenagers collected in one slim volume, and published by NDGC Publishing Ltd (£79.99, but hell it's good). This is the first collection of its kind and provides final proof, if it were needed, that teenagers are horrible until they want something from you, in which case they can be nice for a bit. The facts and figures are based on all the teenagers that would have been polled if only they could have got out of bed, but it's all true anyway:

Household Chores

- Twelve out of every ten teenagers — that's a whopping 120 per cent! — say they will put their plate in the dishwasher *later*.
- Number of teenagers for whom 'later' means 'never': that same whopping 120 per cent!

- Most common response of teenager when told that 'later' means 'never' and you're not having it, and you're fed up with doing everything round here so DO IT NOW: 'Ruin my life, why don't you?'
- Number of teenagers who equate being requested to perform a household chore — just the one — with having their life ruined: that same whopping 120 per cent.
- Number of towels in family bathroom at beginning of week: 6.
- Number of towels in family bathroom at end of week: 0.
- Number of towels in teenager's bedroom at end of week: 6.
- Percentage of teenagers who say they will return the towels to the bathroom *later*: that same whopping 120 per cent!

Most Common Teenage Sayings

You've ruined my life. Get out my face. Alex's mum lets him stay out until 1 a.m. I *would* have called but I didn't have any credit. I do have credit but I didn't want to waste it on you. Yes, I know I *said* I was going to Molly's but *now* I'm at Katie's. My stupid, dumb hair! That's so, like, not fair. It's not my fault. I'm not lying! I *can* go out looking like this. I'm not a child any more. It wasn't me. You're such a nag. Oh, whoopee, Grandma's on a Saturday night (must be said with a great deal of sarcasm). I would have been home in time but Alice wasn't feeling well, so I had to sit with her for several days. Why do I have to go to Grandma's? But if I miss the party my life might as well be over, finished with. Sorry, I forgot. I hate you. Shut up. So what if we haven't seen Grandma for ages? I might as well be in prison. I *have* turned the sound down. You're so mean. Mummy, love you, love you, love you, can you pick me up/lend me a tenner/take me into town? Daddy, love you, love you, love you, can *you* pick me up/lend me a tenner/take me into town? *Later* — I'll do it *later*.

Appearance

- Percentage of teenage girls who must — *must* — stay home from school because their hair won't go right: 100.
- Typical response of teenage girl whose mother says, 'You look fine to me': 'What do you know, bozo? Your hair hasn't looked right since 1963, and even then it was weird.'
- Best description of a teenage girl's ability to go into Topshop on Tuesday and come out a week on Thursday, having bought a top that is exactly like all her other tops: absolutely phenomenal.
- Average number of times a day that the teenage boy

checks for hair in places he didn't have hair before but should have by now because he imagines that everybody else does: 7,896.

· Number of years teenage boy will use Lynx (Africa) before realising his mother was right to gag all these years — it *is* vile: four (age 13 to 17 years).

School

The top ten teen excuses for performing badly or misbehaving at school are:

1) Who cares about physics anyway? It's just so gay.
2) It's only because Miss Bradley picks on me.
3) I can't revise because I left the book in school.
4) I don't care if I'm a drop-out. Maybe I *want* to end up working in Comet so I can answer 'Dunno' to customers' queries while yawning.
5) I did remember to bring the book home, but it's the wrong one.
6) I only got a detention because Mr Roper hates me. All the others were doing much worse stuff and he didn't do anything to them.
7) I wasn't there when the homework was set.
8) What letter from the year head? He didn't give it to me. I know you just found it all crumpled up in my wastepaper bin, but I'm as mystified as you are.

9) Yes, I know it appears that all I'm doing is looking at naked girls on the internet, but it is important homework of the kind that might very well take me until 3 a.m. Schools have changed since your day, Mum.

10) Mum, you know that Nelson Mandela project you stayed up all night to do for me because I had four weeks to do it in but only remembered at 11 p.m. the night before it was due in and you said someone had to do it because otherwise I'd end up a loser working in Comet? Well, you got a D. Cheers, Mum. Thanks a lot.

How to Get Them to Behave

The NDGC has this to say about disciplining children. Be very wary of smacking as a way of teaching your child how to behave. Aside from anything else, it doesn't work particularly well. One of the most telling reasons for banning corporal punishment in schools was that the same handful of children were being beaten again and again and so were clearly not 'learning their lesson'. This is why we always advise parents to be a little more imaginative when it comes to discipline. There are many alternatives to smacking children, like tying them up by their ankles in dark cellars or putting them out to work in the Third World stitching footballs. Such punishments are not only more effective, but also make you feel better as a parent for *not* having smacked. However, if you do not wish to resort to any kind of physical response, or you have a bad arm, or cannot recall if the Third World is right at the end of the road or left, there are still many ways to punish a child. The following all work well: do funny dances in front of their friends; kiss them extravagantly in public; wear strange hats and vivid lipstick in public; wear leather (particularly at the school gate); turn up at their parties; turn up at their parties in leather, hat, vivid lipstick; argue violently with referees; get into their music; tuck little love notes into their packed lunches; make them very smelly packed lunches heavily biased towards egg; show your cleavage (tons of it, particularly at parents' evenings); enter beauty contests on holiday; parade in your underwear when their friends are round; get your belly button pierced; call them by an affectionate nickname and ruffle their hair just as you're passing a gang of hoodies; boast about their achievements down the shops; buy condoms as you leave the barber's; kiss them extravagantly in public and then give them several hugs, just for good measure; get a tattoo; get two tattoos; purchase an extremely serious push-up bra just for parents' evenings; kiss them extravagantly in front of their friends while doing a funny dance; discuss your sex life; wear low-waisted jeans and thongs; sit at the back of the bus on school trips, smoking out the window and drinking Dubonnet from a flask; put beetroot in the packed lunch; fall off the bus and be carried home; ask the hoodies if they want to see any baby pictures; every time they mention a child of the opposite sex ask, 'Is that your boy/girlfriend?'; get yet another tattoo; give them a packed lunch that is only beetroot and eggs; follow them around Topshop buying what they buy while complaining loudly about the standard of workmanship.

Of course, there will always be people who will say, 'But I was smacked as a child and it didn't do me any harm.' That's nonsense. Smacking is a terrible thing and can, as I have shown, be easily avoided in ways that leave no scars aside from the mental ones, which are neither here nor there. Lastly, there is never any need to make a child wear a pointy hat with a 'D' on it, but it can be amusing all the same!

An Excellent Parenting Q & A Session
Hosted by the Non-Domestic Goddess Club (GB)

Dear NDGC: *I find it very hard to shift my kids from in front of the television. They'd watch all day if they could and often do. Any advice?*

A: At the beginning of every week go through the TV listings with them and allow them to pick out one programme a day that they truly want to watch. Write these down on a piece of paper, tape it to the fridge, then totally ignore it because, frankly, the alternative might be having to do something with pipe cleaners and glittery stuff and glue. Do not feel bad about yourself as a lot of what's on television these days is very educational. Indeed, as one boy said to his mother as she was doing the laundry: 'Mum, why don't you use Ace? It's tough on stains but kind enough for delicates.' And you know what? That mother *did* use Ace and she *did* find it tough on stains but kind enough for delicates. The thing about children is that they can often teach you almost as much as you can teach them, but not quite because you are the grown-up and can simply say, when pressed, 'Because I say so.' But never say, 'Don't waste tissues, just use your sleeve,' as this is playing right into their hands.

Dear NDGC: *My child is desperate for a pet but I am not so sure, mainly because I am convinced that once the novelty has worn off I will be left to look after it. Do you think pets are good for children?*

A: You are right to be worried, but have you thought of Sea Monkeys? Sea Monkeys come in a box showing them snorkelling and scuba diving and sitting on thrones wearing crowns and little flippers and sometimes there are even pirate ones with patches over one eye and wooden legs and cutlasses. Now, there is nothing to match the disappointment on a child's face once he or she realises that there are no flippers or snorkels or thrones or cutlasses or even monkeys, just slimy grey flecks that, should they thrive at all, will eat each other as well as their own poo. In our experience, your child will rightly soon lose interest, in which case you can chuck the whole lot down the waste disposal unit while grinding

on max and whistling a merry tune because, apart from anything else, they're repulsive and make you feel sick. This should stop them ever hankering for a pet again. (If not, remember: hamsters and fish can also go down the waste disposal unit but never put a cat down without chopping it up first as it can choke the system.)

Dear NDGC: *My pre-teen daughter would like to have a sleepover for her birthday but I've heard that they can be a nightmare: tears; explosive rows about who sleeps where; finally asleep by 4.59 a.m. and up again at 5 a.m., trampolining on the mattresses; more tears . . . any sleepover tips?*

A: Yes. Don't. Ever.

Dear NDGC: *My young child would like a TV in her bedroom but I am against it. What do you think?*

A: Apparently, 42 per cent of toddlers now have televisions in their bedrooms. We find that statistic truly shocking. I mean, what are the parents of the other 58 per cent thinking of? Come on, we live in the First World! Get a grip!

Children: The Real, Real Facts

Dear NDGC: *I recently read that the cost of amusing a child over the summer holidays is, on average, £1,200, what with tennis camps and new toys and so on. However, there is no way I can afford this much, so I wonder if you have any ideas for entertaining them that cost nothing or next to nothing?*

A: You've got us here as We're all for throwing money at kids to get them out from under your feet. Have you tried, perhaps, hide and seek in which they hide and you somehow forget to seek? This can keep them behind the sofa or in a cupboard for a week, sometimes more, and, apart from the rehydrating fluids, needn't cost a penny. Alternatively, how about turning the situation to your advantage and getting your child into shoplifting? This is something they will probably have to do on their own initially but later they could join a gang. It is always good for a child, and essential for their self-esteem, to feel part of a gang. And, who knows, he or she may later graduate to stealing cars to order. If so, do let us know, as it's extremely likely we could put some business their way.

Dear NDGC: *Do you agree that boredom is the greatest gift you can give a child?*

A: The trouble with boredom is that it is really quite boring. A telly in the bedroom is better.

Dear NDGC: *I have a good career and a beautiful house but I'm getting on a bit and worry if I don't have a child now I never will, which I might regret. On the other hand, I just don't know if I'm ready for it. How can I know?*

A: A: OK, here goes. First, smear peanut butter and mud all over your hands and then wipe them on the curtains, carpets and walls. You may wish to crayon all over them at the same time. Next, get a piece of toast and stuff it in the video player while dragging the cat around by its tail and squashing bananas into the sofa cushions. Make sure you get up 27 times a night to swing a Moses basket and sing every song you have ever heard and some you haven't. Take your breasts out in public. Spend all of Christmas Day constructing a Playmobil castle which, the moment it's up, will start to deconstruct itself such that, even years later, you cannot go to the toilet in the middle of the night without kebabing your foot on a medieval maiden's pointy hat. Put a tea-towel on your partner's head, pretend he is a shepherd in a nativity play and clap rapturously even if he forgets his words and then cries and then wets his pants and then complains about not being able to hold 'Little Baby Cheesy'. Practise saying, 'Put a jumper on. It is cold out there.' Don't practise saying, 'Well, if it's OK with Alex's mum, it's OK with me,' as that would be playing right into their hands. This is how to tell if you are ready.

Dear NDGC: *Should I just buy a two-bed flat in St John's Wood instead?*

A: You bet.

3

High Days
and Holidays

The School Holidays are Holidays for Whom, Exactly?

E very now and then the schools will close and will not re-open until a specified time, no matter how hard you pound on the doors or rap on the windows. We at the Club understand this but would still like to say: 'These periods can last from one week through to six, which is unbelievable considering how dumb children are and, therefore, how much schooling they need. In fact, it would make a lot more sense to keep children in school at all times with the option of a half-day on Christmas Day should the parents feel up to it, which is by no means a given.' Alternatively, it is wise to kick off any school holiday with some good ground rules. This may involve putting posters up around the house with the following slogans:

Do Not Ask for Credit as Refusal Often Offends

I am Not a Taxi

The Specials Today are 'Take It' or 'Leave It'

I am Not an ATM

Don't Use That Tone with Me

The Specials Tomorrow will be 'Take It' or 'Leave It'

What Part of 'No' Didn't You Understand?

The Specials will be 'Take It' or 'Leave It' into Perpetuity, so There is No Point in Even Asking, Is There?'

Then again, there are all those 'activities' you could ferry them to and from if you were a taxi, but you're not. Honestly, the trouble with today's kids is that they expect judo and swimming and football and guitar and going to Tom's house and, therefore, do not stay in watching TV and playing on the PlayStation enough. What do you think we bought the TV and the PlayStation for? To gather dust? You may be seduced into a trip out to any of the following places, but don't say you haven't been warned.

The Indoor Playcentre: These have names like 'Clowntown', 'Monkey Business' or 'Pirates Playhouse' and will smell of Monster Munch, pee and feet. The coffee with taste of Monster Munch, pee and feet. The tea will also taste of Monster Munch, pee and feet. The coffe and tea will therefore be indistinguishable. Still, they are ideal for children who need to let off steam so long as the parents can endure the Monster Munch, pee and feet ambiance, which very few can.

The Art Café: These are the places where the children paint ceramics which are later fired. They are excellent value for money if you don't factor in that a side plate can mysteriously transmute into a £70 bill. They can also provide a good afternoon's entertainment, particularly for Control-Freak Mum, who is surely in her element. It is: 'Not that colour!' And: 'You're ruining it!' And: 'You obviously don't know anything about a ballerina's correct proportions!' And: 'Oh, give it here!' The Non-Control-Freak Mum won't bother to pick up the ceramics once they have been fired, making it even better value for money.

The Park: It's free, it's healthy, and once the boys have robbed you of your coat and jumper for goalposts, you can freeze on a bench while wishing you were dead, and the sooner the better.

The Family Day Out: This is often promoted as a lovely thing to do even though what amuses one family member rarely amuses another. While one is thinking 'The London Eye' another might be thinking 'The Globe' while yet another is thinking about a theme park like Chessington World of Asbos where the *faux* Burberry count is always blisteringly high and you may well overhear one teenage boy saying to another, 'Effing 'ell, that ride was well spasticating.' (Excuse me, if you are going to spasticate, may I suggest you do it elsewhere?) So the family day out will pan out like this: the one who wanted World of Asbos sulks, the one who wanted the Globe sulks, the one who wanted the London Eye might have got her way but she also sulks because everyone else is ruining it by sulking. The biggest sulker is usually World of Asbos who, once cattle-prodded on to the Eye, will *only* look at the floor. And then there is the gift shop. At the end of a family day out there is always a gift shop at the exit, filled with the worst rubbish imaginable: novelty erasers; novelty pencils; novelty paperweights; novelty sweatshirts and all manner of themed rip-offs. The younger child will wail for all of it, in which case we would suggest saying, firmly but fairly, 'Here's a tenner. Get what you want so long as you don't cry all the way home.' Should a tenner not be enough, up it to twenty. The other thing about family days out is that they can be expensive.

Christmas: What's the Big Deal?

Christmas. Nothing to it. Getting stressed at Christmas is for losers. It's only, after all, a roast dinner and a few gifts. It's fine. Why do people get so het up? Come on, love, it happens every year. Same time, same place, nothing new in it, get a grip. The shopping is not *that* bad. It's only shopping. Shopping, shopping, shopping. And then more shopping. And yet more shopping. And then just when you think, at last I have finished the shopping, there will be some more shopping. And that will be the last bit of shopping until the next bit of shopping, which will also be the last bit of shopping until the next bit of shopping, and so it's rather like a race to see which is going to give up first, your money or your feet? True, it's all very well when they expire together but it can turn ugly when your feet have had it, say, but your credit card is still criminally up for it

and goes, 'Come on, feet, it's only yet more
shopping,' and the feet say, 'Look, why don't you just
piss off?' and this can be very embarrassing, especially
if it happens on the bus, because you then have to say
to everybody, 'Please excuse my feet. It's just that
they're so bushed.' But none of it is anything to get
stressed about: same time, same place; nothing new
in it. Getting stressed at Christmas is for losers,
although there is, of course, the waking at 4 a.m. with

heart pounding and mind racing with all sorts of last-minute considerations like, 'Bread sauce? What is all that about then?' and 'The turkey, I'm sure it's too small', and 'The turkey, I'm sure it's too big to fit in the oven', and 'Did I really need to spend 82 quid on an organic, free-range Kelly bird just because Nigella recommended it?' 82 quid, 82 quid! Oh, I'm all for free-range and organic and treating animals well, but what did these ones have? En-suite with DVD? If I'd wanted to spend that much on a Kelly bird couldn't I have got Lorraine, who would probably feed 97 and look at the breast on it, for heaven's sake. Tuck in, everybody! Tuck in! AND WHO'S GOT THE SELLOTAPE? WHO'S GOT THE SCISSORS? All I am saying is that these are the sorts of things *some* people can get quite worked up about.

Anyway, it's all about the kids, really, and Christmas is much better with kids because at least then you have someone to take the stress out on, if you are the sort of loser who gets stressed by this sort of thing. But you'd still like to give them something of a magical time so it's stocking fillers, stocking fillers, stocking fillers and damn the Scalextric which won't work unless you spend an hour fiddling with the little brushes under the cars and damn the MP3 with the instructions most loosely translated from the original Korean ('Pause now you are in shortly, stop')

and damn the middle of the night, when you wake
with your heart pounding and your mind racing and
oh, God, I'd better get something for her because she
might get something for me but then if she doesn't
get something for me it will be embarrassing having
gotten something for her but is that more
embarrassing than her having got something for me
when I haven't got anything for her and damn those
kids with their questions like, 'Mummy, why does
Father Christmas always use the same wrapping paper
as you?' because while all NDGs are all for giving kids
a magical time, can't they see how tired we are? That
we are practically dropping? That we've had it? Oh
no, carol singers at the door. 'Look, just go away, you
bobble-hatted loons. Can't you see how tired we are?
That we're practically dropping? Do you want the dog
set on you?' And then it's the wrapping, wrapping,
wrapping and WHO'S GOT THE SELLOTAPE?
WHO'S GOT THE SCISSORS? And then it's
your little nephew on the phone who is four and
better on the phone than he used to be when your
sister would say, 'Oh, just talk to Fred a moment, he
won't talk back but he will listen,' and Fred says he is
going to leave out a mince pie for Santa and so you
say, 'Oh no, Freddie, Santa is very fed up of mince
pies but do you know what he'd really like? He'd like
a barrel of hand-peeled shallots, that's what he'd

really like . . .' and an hour later your sister phones back and shouts, 'Bitch!' and then hangs up, as anyone who has taken the morning off work to peel the one shallot will understand but then she shouldn't have put her littlest one on the phone before he could speak, should she? But the trouble with people who get stressed by Christmas is that they can turn quite nasty. Or so we have heard.

And then there's yet more wrapping, wrapping, wrapping and WHO HAS GOT THE SCISSORS? WHO HAS GOT THE SELLOTAPE? And the things from Amazon that haven't yet arrived and are there enough crackers and is there any point marzipanning the cake as everyone will just pick it off anyway and wouldn't it be nice if my feet and my credit card stopped fighting, fighting, fighting, if only for a minute — Stop it, guys! — and at what point is it acceptable to buy people any old rubbish just for the sheer relief of crossing them off your list and is it around now and what 7-year-old doesn't want a new mop anyway and I'm not crying, it's just that I've been up since dawn peeling the one shallot . . . See? Nothing to it. A cinch. Getting stressed at Christmas is for losers.

Christmas Stress-Busting Tips for Losers

- Quit your job before the office party. It will save time later.
- Get your stories straight. 'Mummy, why does Father Christmas use the same wrapping paper as you?' 'Because we share the same extremely good taste, darling.'
- Avoid any gadgety shops unless you want your head sliced off by a demo helicopter.
- Goats and honeybees are nice thoughts, but hell to wrap and then hell to keep secret.
- Keep the scissors and Sellotape for your sole use only (if necessary, hide in pants).
- Try not to get too competitive about cards, always eyeing up how many others have received, but it's always sensible to send yourself a good number all the same.

- Gift tokens, gift tokens, gift tokens. (Although they always seem like a feeble present to give in early December, by Christmas Eve they are beginning to look pretty cool.)
- Should a sexual encounter come your way, remove scissors and Sellotape from pants.

How to Write a Christmas Bestseller

If you've yet to have a brilliant and original idea for a little must-have book of the Christmas, bestselling novelty kind, all is not lost. Sometimes the most brilliant and original ideas have already been done, so it's perfectly acceptable to have them long after someone else has while passing them off as your own (in fact, the Club positively encourages such behaviour). A compilation of puzzling queries followed by informed answers, or examples, should fit the bill nicely. Our own is called *Why Do Some People Take Forever at the Cashpoint?*, although the following extract may lead to a puzzling query in itself: where are the informed answers? Well, in these instances you, the readers, are expected to respond with the informed answers, thereby making this idea the most brilliant of brilliant ideas; in effect, you write the book while NDGC Publishing Ltd cash in. Any informed answers to any of the following queries will be gratefully received, although you'd be foolish to expect a cut. Ill-informed answers are also acceptable.

Why do some people take forever at the cashpoint?

Why do people who work in health food shops always look so sickly?

If I could somehow time travel back to the Big Bang and the moment of creation, would I have anywhere to watch it from?

If you put a humidifier and a dehumidifier in the same room and left them to fight it out, which one would win?

While it is not uncommon to hear someone coughing in their sleep, how come I've never heard anybody sneeze?

Why does bottled water have a 'best by' date on it?

Why are men who carry their change in little coin purses always so spooky and impossible to take seriously?

Why do two little white lines appear in the corner of a television programme just before the ad break?

If you can't teach an old dog new tricks, how come Woofie, our lovely ancient Labrador, recently worked his way though Marvyn's First Magic Box and put on a wonderful show?

Why do poor people on benefits always have such big televisions?

As a dog has a very developed sense of smell, and smell is linked to taste, does a dog also have a very developed sense of taste? (And if so, does it think, 'Oh no, not the same bloody stuff from a tin again,' at every meal?)

Can lactose ever be people-intolerant?

Who planted the first seedless grape?

Why does the Inland Revenue pursue people even when they live by the seaside?

What distinguishes a satsuma from a clementine, a clementine from a mandarin, a mandarin from a tangerine and which is the best?

Why is the fluff in the tumble drier always grey (no matter the colour of the wash)?

Does that Kerry person ever look at her spread from Iceland and think, 'Bloody hell, look at all the crap in that. I wish I'd spent the extra and gone to Marks.'

If in the TV show *Quincy*, when the DA said, 'Suicide!' and Quincy said, 'Murder!' and they then had a bit of a head-to that went as follows, without variation:

QUINCY: 'Murder.'
DA: 'Suicide.'
QUINCY: 'Murder.'
DA: 'Suicide.'

. . . was Quincy always right or was he ever, ever wrong?

Just one cow's milk but so many cheeses. How does that work?

Why is it that the people in the Ferrero Rocher television commercials never speak for us all by saying, 'I hate to rain on your parade, ambassador, but you're actually not spoiling us at all with these chocolates, so wholly non-exclusive you can get them down the garage, and it doesn't even have to be a nice garage, as even those ones where you have to pay the man through a grille appear to stock them in obscene amounts. Share the magic this Christmas, my arse.'

Why does a teenager who finally wears his parents down begging and re-begging for a mobile phone then never answer it?

If the Earth spins on its axis and completes one rotation every 24 hours, then it follows that people at the Equator will travel a far greater distance than those at the Poles, in which case: do people at the Equator say 'Are we there yet?' more often than those nearer the Poles?

Why do washing machines come with so many programmes when no one uses more than one — maybe 'D', which seems as good as any — and to hell with the consequences?

Why is it that the more clothes worn by a toddler — coat, dungarees, jumper over dungarees, tights, pants, pants under tights, pants on top of tights — the more likely they are to not only need to be taken to a public toilet but, after several hours spent disrobing them, will do one whispery fart, exclaim 'Finished!' and then wonder why you re-dress them so brusquely? (Don't get me started on snowsuits.)

Would cows thrive on human breast milk?

Why was a squirrel chosen as a symbol of the Tufty Club when its own road-safety record is hardly glowing.

What sort of person is sad enough to read to the end of complete and utter nonsense such as this?

Is this the perfect gift for someone you don't like very much? (You bet!)

Mother's Day

This is a first-hand account of one mother's Mother's Day.

Now, while it is true that this mother has suffered some disappointments in the past, she doesn't want to put pressure on the family to shower her with lovely treats on this day. After all, it's only the one day in the calendar exclusively for mothers; your mother, the woman who has done everything for you ever since you were born and who is generally smashing, even if she says so herself, which she often does. 'I'm smashing, I am,' she will say. 'Do you even have any idea what a smashing mother you have?' Still, she doesn't want to put any pressure on anyone to acknowledge just how smashing she is and, as such, who exactly puts up all the notices that appear all over the house in the preceding days — 'Mothers' Day: One Week to Go!', 'Mothers' Day: Only Two

Shopping Days Left!', 'I am Not a Taxi' (left over
from half-term) — is anyone's guess. As it happens,
the mother wishes that whoever is doing it would stop.
In particular, she feels that using a laundry pen to
mirror-write on her child's forehead — 'Mother's
Day: Not Another Pasta Calendar, If It's All the Same
to You!' — while he is asleep is taking it too far. If
there is to be a gift, the mother isn't picky. It's the
thought that counts, although sometimes the mother
has thought about the thought and, while she accepts
that thoughts do count, they are never quite as good
as a present. The mother thinks anything will do so
long as it is given with love — or at least isn't too
rubbish. The mother can recall being small and
buying her own mother *A Thousand Recipes for the Freezer*
from W.H. Smith in the days when W.H. Smith did
what it was supposed to do and didn't try to sell you a
half-price chocolate orange at the till. This mother
does not want *A Thousand Recipes for the Freezer*, or indeed
A Thousand Recipes for Anywhere, because the mother feels
that if the family are not accustomed to her cooking
the same four things over and over from *The Resentful
Kitchen*, then they only have themselves to blame.
They've had lots of time to get used to it. This mother
often thinks, 'Thank God for pasta with pesto,' and,
'Thank God for pasta without pesto,' and that's two
of the recipes for you, and you can take it or leave it

as there is nothing else on offer today. The mother also does not want a foot spa. That said, though, the mother did receive a foot spa once and was very impressed by the remote control which she thought would be handy should she be in one room and her feet in another.

The mother suspects that if a spontaneous gift is forthcoming then the father will probably have to fund it, as the son spends all his money on chips from the chippy and panini from the bakery, even though the money could be better spent on the mother, who is smashing. The mother doesn't understand why he has to buy all those chips when he can always get pasta with pesto or pasta without pesto at home. It just doesn't make sense to her. Whatever, the mother thinks that all hints in the gift department are probably best directed at the father. Happily, the mother finds a page in a glossy magazine showing the top must-have handbags. The mother thinks this is a good place to start, although she doesn't really get must-have handbags (which you must have or what? Your guts will explode out of your ears?) The mother puts her hand over the price of the 'Joni' by 'Luella' and asks the father to guess how much. The mother, who, aside from being smashing also has a great sense of humour that is never cruel or mocking, knows this will be a laugh. The father says, 'Well, it looks cheap,

but you wouldn't ask if it wasn't expensive . . . £35?'
The mother agrees that the more expensive a bag is
the cheaper it looks. This is something she doesn't get
either. But still. She shows the father the price. The
price of a 'Joni' is £4,720. The father gasps and says,
'You could get a Daewoo Matiz for that.' The mother
does not tell the father he is always showing himself
up by knowing all about the cheapest things you can
buy, or that she can't imagine anyone on their
deathbed thinking: 'I wish I'd bought a Daewoo
Matiz,' but would like you to know what she has to live
with all the same. The mother does not think she'll be
getting the 'Joni', which is, apparently, available from
Harrods even though it looks as if it came out of a
New Look bargain bin.

So now it is Mother's Day, which kicks off rather
late because the mother is determined to enjoy her
surprise breakfast in bed, and so lies there waiting for
it until just after 5 p.m. She is sorry to ruin the
surprise by getting up just after 5 p.m., but thinks
that if she lies in bed any longer she will not be able
to get up at all without fainting. Some mothers may
have thought, 'They could have managed a croissant
between them. How hard is that?' But this mother
doesn't have a resentful bone in her body and if, say,
she was to forget to tape the football next time they
ask, who could blame her, what with her memory

being what it is? Still, in the end she does get a lovely present – 'A pasta calendar, thank you, darling!' – as well as a home-made card (even though one of those notices she had put up had read 'Mother's Day: Shops *sell* cards as well, you know!', but she is strangely pleased to get it all the same, and it's no more than she deserves. She's smashing, she is. Even if she says so herself. Repeatedly.

We're All Going on a Summer Holiday, More Fool Us

Listen, why stay at home not getting on when you can all drive thousands of miles across France to spend two weeks together not getting on? You know it makes sense. It's tempting to go on separate holidays but, alas, the kids will always find you in the end. Here are the things no child has ever been heard to say on holiday:

'I could sit in the back of this car for ever.'

'What a lovely view!'

'I'll just write that postcard to Grandma.'

'Please could you suncream me? I will stand very still. Oops, I think you have missed a bit there.'

'I've probably had enough ice-cream for one day.'

'Any chance of fitting in a medieval church this afternoon?'

'I've run out of books to read.'

'I'm bushed; I think I'll turn in and leave you adults to it.'

'I feel like a shower.'

'I'll just unpack and put everything carefully away. (Did you bring the fragranced drawer-liners?)'

'I'll just write another postcard to Grandma; you know how Grandma loves postcards.'

'Oh, no. Not another water park.'

'I'll be in in a minute; I've just got to brush all this sand off.'

'Is it OK if I hang my trunks out to dry?'

And, of course: 'I'll get it, Mum; it's your holiday, too.'

So, the Truth about Summer Holidays, Then

First, there is the **packing**. In the run-up to holiday time women's magazines — don't men *ever* pack? — will make a big deal of this. They will be full of 'How to Pack' features as if it's rocket science, which even we thought it was until we asked a passing rocket scientist, who said there weren't as many similarities as we are given to think. Often, these features have been written by a 'lifestyle consultant' who knows what they're talking about, having had many years of experience fleecing people who should know better. The lifestyle consultant will talk about tissue paper and 'basics' and taking 'appropriate accessories' — what, I won't need a balaclava in the tropics? — whereas what it comes down to is this: Get a bag. Throw some stuff in it. If it won't close, take some stuff out. If it now closes easily, put some of the stuff you've just taken out back in. Fret about what to take

by all means, but as you'll probably only wear the one
thing over and over, what's the point? This is the way
it will be this year, next year and the year after that.
This is just the way it is. Get over it. (Things no
lifestyle consultant has ever been heard to say, at least
not until the cheque has been banked and cleared:
'Just get a life, why don't you?')

Naturally, you must leave room in any bag for the
souvenirs you will wish to bring home. These will
surely include at least one item that seemed like a
good idea at the time but, on your return, will make
you sit on the edge of your bed and ask gaspingly,
'What was I thinking of?' Chances are it's a shell-
fringed sarong in an electric-blue, swimming-fish
print, so handy for Asda, the school run and putting
the rubbish out. It will also make the most appalling,
shell-clacking din. Post on eBay without delay, even
though the chances of ever getting rid of it are almost
nil as everyone has their own shell-clacking sarong
or similar. (Should you miraculously get a bid,
although it might be fair to point out the garment's
unsuitability you are not obliged to do so.)

Now, on to the trickiest matter of all: the
swimsuit. In a mad moment of pre-holiday euphoria
you will likely be seduced by a swimsuit that is not
only completely unbefitting but will make you the
laughing stock of all other holidaymakers. It may have

a large 'O' cut out in the middle (oh, for God's sake), or it may be one of those shorts-legs jobs that make you look like Popeye, only less attractive and more masculine, with a sort of flesh explosion in the thigh area. Quite why you made this purchase is anyone's guess. Did you think your thighs would magically disappear on the way to the airport? That your cellulite would get off the Tube before Heathrow – at Turnham Green, for example – and say, 'See you in two weeks. Have a good time.' Even your own partner may disloyally laugh at you. 'Here comes Popeye,' he might say, before falling off his sun lounger in hysterics. You may choose to wear the swimsuit – teamed with the balaclava, which you bought along anyway – to bed. That'll put paid to any thoughts he might have of holiday sex. You may or may not wish to add a snorkel and flippers.

If you are flying and travelling to the airport by **minicab** it is, of course, wise to imply that the house has not been left empty. Good things to say might include, 'It was nice of Vinnie Jones to offer to house-sit for us.' Or, 'I hope we have left enough food out for our Rottweiler, Killer, who has really, really sharp teeth.' Or, 'I do hope Les Dennis will be all right on his own. Maybe someone will break in so he can talk to them non-stop about his past marital difficulties such that they won't be able to get away for the next fortnight at least.' And remember: wherever you are flying from, to whatever destination, you will always leave by the very furthest **gate**. It may even be gate 876. That's just the way it is. Take sandwiches.

And, Lastly, Halloween

This is the ancient pagan festival of turning off all the lights, hiding behind the sofa, pretending not to be in and not answering the door under any circumstances. Therefore, your essential checklist should read as follows. Have I:

1) turned off all the lights;
2) hidden behind the sofa;
3) pretended to not be in;
4) vowed not to answer the door under any circumstances?

That should cover it.

4

Health and Fitness

We know it is very important to be fit and healthy and go to the gym and not smoke and not drink. We know this is very important even though unfit, unhealthy people who smoke and drink and do not go to the gym are always the most interesting people in the room. Those who do yoga are fine, but why does it never occur to them that once you have emptied your mind it might be a good idea to refill it? Alternative therapists are fine, too, although it is very hard to get them to accept alternative methods of payment. Have you ever tried to pay an alternative therapist alternatively? As one Club member recounts: 'I recently tried to pay an aromatherapist alternatively, with an old shoe, and she wasn't having any of it. "I don't accept old shoes," she said, throwing it after me. So I not only left more stressed than when I went in — so much for all that yarrow and

clary sage — but also with a graze over my left eye where the old shoe had caught me! I was minded to pop back in for some ylang-ylang and bergamot oil, which is said to be good for wounds, but thought better of it when I saw my alternative, alternative method of payment — a Cornish pasty with just the one bite out of it — being thrown out after me, too.'
We don't know why alternative therapists have to be so conventional in this respect, but guess that if they didn't complement their ancient ways of doing things with the most up-to-date computerised billing systems then it wouldn't be complementary medicine.

Detox? Yes, detox by all means, but retoxing is, we believe, much more fun as you can eat a great deal of cake and even accelerate the smoking, doing it where you otherwise wouldn't, like in the shower, down into babies' cots and up Paul McKenna's trouser leg.

Ah, Smoking...

Smoking is a thing that smokers do time after time during the day — and sometimes in the night, if they get up for a pee, as why waste the opportunity? — because they like it so much. Sometimes smokers think they shouldn't smoke because they don't want to die of that cancer which means you have to have an oxygen tank in the hall, even though you are dying on the sofa in the other room or upstairs in bed. Every New Year — New Year, New You! — smokers try to stop smoking but it is hard because smoking has become a kind of punctuation; life's full stops and commas and colons. Without it, everything gets all jumbled up, just as a language would without grammar, and you can go quite mad and will certainly get totally furious about everything. The fury may even be the defining thing. Ask smokers how the not smoking is going and they will say something like this.

How is the Not Smoking Going?

'Oh . . . fine, thank you, if you don't count these queasy feelings I get about the rest of my life stretching before me in an utterly empty and meaningless way and the fizzing fury. Actually, it's not that bad. The only things that make me really furious are pizza leaflets and minicab cards and people who spit in the street and the dirty dishes stacked by the dishwasher (would it kill you to put them in?) and hard-boiled eggs that won't give up their shells without a fight and clean dishes never unstacked from the dishwasher (would it kill you to take them out?) and God (what did he invent tobacco for?) and packaging you have to open with your teeth and the person ahead of you in the supermarket who looks surprised at being asked to pay and spends forever rummaging in her handbag for her purse and litter-droppers and people who go on about "cool camping" when there is nothing "cool" about camping and the council who makes us fastidiously separate everything for recycling and then throws it all in the back of the same truck and TV dramas in which everyone is smoking and so you want to suck the screen . . . Do I seem irritable to you?'

New Year, New You?

Yes, yes. The Club knows it has to be done. At the end of the year everybody says so. The newspapers say so. Women's magazines say so. 'New Year, New You!' they say. It's what we are all meant to be thinking about. There may even be an accompanying photograph of a woman in Lycra running along a beach, abundantly glowing with health and fitness and vitality and the kind of positive attitude that makes it possible to achieve all your goals and those of a few other people and you know that if you were to cut her she would bleed Evian. And this is who you want to be.

And why not? After all, it's only about tweaking who you already are to become someone else entirely. The Old You will initially say it wants the New You very much indeed. 'Bring it on,' the Old You will say. The Old You did go jogging the once, and almost got to the corner, but the Old You's thighs rubbed together so vigorously she nearly set her underpants on fire. Don't get the Old You started on chapping.

The Old You, with all its dirty habits, is entirely fed up of itself. The Old You is genuinely looking forward to getting its marching orders from the New You, although it seriously wonders if it is even up to marching. The Old You's current fitness level means it cannot even whip cream without having to take small, panting breaks slumped against the fridge. This may then bring on the need to lie down, perhaps for an hour, but possibly for longer if *Trisha* is on and then *Flog It* and then *Des and Mel*, all of which can distract from becoming a better person and achieving personal goals as well as impersonal ones and making more progress at work. The Old You's whipped cream is never as whipped as it could be. The Old You's trifle is more like soup. The Old You has achieved some local fame with her trifle, which is said to be quite unlike anyone else's.

The Old You prepares for 1 January and the arrival of the New You with a great deal of excitement as well as vast amounts of eating, drinking, smoking and being inert. The Old You knows that the New You is not going to put up with any of that nonsense so it's best to cram in as much of it as possible now. The New You is going to give the Old You a good kick up

the arse, which it will not be able to miss. There are
goals and goals, and the Old You's arse, most would
agree, is an open one and not worth bragging about
in the event you are on target, which you will be if you
are on the same continent. You may even still be on
target if you are not on the same continent. If you
are, though, you are welcome to drop in for a nice
drink of trifle.

So, the Old You will go to bed on New Year's Eve.
The Old You will be quite drunk, as ever, and will
have eaten excessively while taking no exercise, unless
you count the distance between the fridge and the
TV, which can actually mount up. Sometimes, the
Old You can be a little too hard on itself. But it's
OK, because, come morning, the New You will have
arrived and it'll all be beaches and running and
vitality and Evian and moving yourself forward
towards a more satisfying existence, both personally
and professionally as recommended by life coaches.
(But rarely by National Express coaches. It's wise to
know there is a difference between the two, as you
don't want to sign up for a series of confidential
sessions exploring what's been holding you back all
these years when your only true aim is to get to
Brighton, returning on the same day.)

Come New Year's Day, the New You will definitely
want to go running at 6.30 a.m., so that's what time

the alarm is set for. But when it goes off, what happens? What invariably happens is this: the Old You, who has so happily played along until now, has been so optimistic about the possibility of real change, acts like an only child who is presented with a sibling and basically tells it to go away and mind its own business and weren't we happy, you and I, in our own little toxic and inert way with no goals to bother us? The Old You, you know, would like to put a pillow over New You's face or, if not, at least pinch it on the arm really, really hard and then say, 'It wasn't me!'

As it is, the Old You sits on the New You, pinning it down, so that you cannot get out of bed to go for that run no matter how hard you try, which may not be very hard at all. Still, the New You doesn't put up much of a fight. It turns out the New You wouldn't say boo to a goose. Ultimately, you have no alternative but to turn over and go directly back to sleep and then, by the time you wake up at, say, noonish, there is no sign of the New You whatsoever; no thought of a run. What a loser the New You annually turns out to be. Thank God, in fact, for the Old You, which has stuck by you all these years, through thick and thick as, if you are like us, you don't do thin.

You know, in all these years of 'New Year, New You!', you've probably never even seen New You's face. It's not the Old You that always fails you. It's the New one. As for two litres of Evian a day, and as the Old You will constantly point out, it has its dangers, particularly as it can give you the sort of 'full' feeling that can otherwise be achieved with cake. Lots and lots and lots of cake.

And the Not Smoking?

'Well, little gets to me now, unless you count: free rubbish CD compilations; family members who bite the cheese straight from the fridge; the pigs; Lindsey Bareham's *Just One Pot* cookbook that uses lots of pots to get to the one pot stage, the bitch; traffic wardens; people who take for ever at the cashpoint (what are they doing?); the person who rummages at the supermarket and finally comes up with a cheque book and 72 assorted money-off coupons; Paul McKenna's *Quit Smoking Easily Right Now*, because there is no easy way to quit smoking right now, you wanker; the Rausing family who have made so much money from a product that doesn't work, go figure; pedestrians on zebra crossings who fail to make any thank-you gesture when you stop for them, so forcing you to wind down the window and shout, "Don't mention it, mate"; your partner retrieving the free CDs of rubbish compilations from the rubbish and saying you can't just throw away CDs so you're going to have to learn

to live with Female Legends *Vol. 1*; Nigerians who want
your help transferring monies; teenage boys claiming
the computer for urgent school work of the kind that
turns out to involve looking at pictures of naked girls
until midnight; the website you registered with years
ago to find out one thing and you're still paying
£7.99 a month for; those New Year fitness
resolutions you know you'll never stick
to . . .'

Come on, People Can Change

Really? OK, here is a report on someone's New Year, New You! health and fitness progress so far. This person is called 'Deborah' but is no relation to the author of this book and anyone who suggests otherwise will be hearing from her solicitor and her mother who takes these things very seriously.

General Attitude: D

Deborah certainly has an attitude problem. Some members of her household, for example, enjoy Channel 4's *You are What You Eat* and feel they have much to learn from it, but Deborah is noisy and disruptive throughout, calling Dr Gillian McKeith a slag and a cow and a bitch and a stringy old witch with a mouth as meanly puckered as a dog's bottom. Deborah gets particularly riled when Dr McKeith opens a kitchen cupboard and exclaims, more or less,

'Crisps! Crisps! Why don't you just reverse over your children in an HGV? Why don't you just inject poison directly into their veins? Why don't you just push them off a cliff on to upturned spikes?' At this point, Deborah always shouts out, 'For God's sake, it's only crisps!' We feel that Deborah is exceedingly immature not just for her age, but for any age. If Deborah had yet to be born she would still be immature for her age. She will have to take drastic action if she is to improve her grades this term. However, on a more positive note, she can recognise shapes and order objects by size.

Exercise: E –
Although Deborah promised she would really work at this and actually get off her backside we have seen little improvement, if any. Deborah participates in anything but. Her resolution — which we discussed with her fully — to go for a run every morning hasn't resulted in a single run. Once. And that even though she bought the fancy trainers, we feel not much progress will be made until she learns to regard the snooze button as less of a friend and more of an enemy. It pains us to say it, but she really would be a total waste of space if only she didn't take up so much of it. As it is, she spends most of her time lying on the sofa, eating lethal crisps and watching telly, just as she

did last term. We would like to say that her contributions to family discussions are, at least, thoughtful and demonstrate an ability to communicate ideas clearly, but, alas, we cannot, as her comments rarely rise above, 'Is Tess Daley the poor man's Cat Deeley, or is it the other way round?' And, 'Couldn't they merge as Tess Deeley as who would know, anyway?' At one point she even begged her teenage son to make her go for a run, but the one time he said, 'Come on then, Mum,' and tried to pull her off the sofa she punched him and told him he was really, really annoying. At the end of last term Deborah said she was serious about this fitness business, and that she was genuinely excited about the possibility of real change, but now it has come to it she is claiming that her Old You is sabotaging her New You, sitting on it, pinning it down, pinching it hard when no one is looking and telling it to shove off. Deborah's behaviour is both wholly unacceptable and a cause for great concern. Still, her written pieces of work this term — especially her essay, 'So, Dr McKeith, What Do You Poo? Pot-pourri?' — almost met the expected level, and you can't honestly say she doesn't have a point.

Diet: U

Deborah really needs to pull her finger out,
particularly when it finds itself in the peanut butter
or box of Celebrations or clawing at the leftover
Christmas pudding which is so fattening she might as
well get herself hooked up to a Trex'n'Cookeen drip
and be done with it. She claims to be working hard at
reducing her alcohol intake, but as she was recently
caught removing the silver-foil pouch from the wine
box and stabbing it with the bread knife to get the
very last squirt out we are not at all convinced. She
said she would do her utmost to drink two litres of
Evian a day but gave up after two sips on the grounds
that 'it is just so tedious'. We believe that if you were
to cut Deborah she would bleed the kind of
caffeine/tobacco/alcohol/cholesterol slick that you'd
never get off birds' wings. It would just be kinder to
break their necks. Meanwhile, her report on
preferring Davina when she was fatter and mumsier
and wore combats was not only an ill-informed and
pathetic exercise in self-justification, it also bored
everyone shitless. I am personally yawning just
thinking about it. If Deborah carries on at this rate,
we feel that she will never fulfil her lifelong ambition
to work in a bank and be sexually harassed. Deborah
says she fails to understand why women who work in
banks and get sexually harassed always make a stink.

Deborah says that if her male boss made lewd and suggestive remarks to her or referred to her as 'eye candy' it would make her day, pretty much. Meanwhile, she can distinguish between different musical rhythms from different cultures and can express herself well during water play. Well done, Deborah!

Appearance: U –

Deborah has neglected to make any improvements in this area. It doesn't help that most of her time is taken up with either leaning on photocopiers, sometimes for several weeks, in the hope of having her bottom pinched, or watching all that telly. Deborah's continually stated belief that Dr McKeith does not have to start every programme with basically saying, 'My, you're fat fuckers, aren't you?' as we can see that for ourselves, is as wearisome as it is offensive to fat fuckers everywhere. We feel Deborah's time would be better spent experimenting with make-up and actually wearing lipstick rather then putting it on and then wiping it off because she feels silly. That said, she does use measuring equipment accurately and is able to draw conclusions from her observations.

Conclusion

This has been a disappointing report all round for Deborah. She has made no progress on any of the above counts and is generally a bad influence, a pain in the arse and has probably put back feminism fifty years. She is useless, irresponsible, does not listen attentively to the opinions of others, leaves tasks incomplete — always — and is horribly selfish, hiding the stuff she likes right at the back of the fridge so no one else can get to it first. We don't think we're alone when we say we wish she was dead and that not much would be lost from the world if she were. She is quite good with sand, though.

You're Heading towards an Early Grave

The Club accepts there are now many
opportunities for good and satisfying careers
in the health and fitness industry, including bullying
fat people on television, while repeating, 'Do you
want to go to an early grave?' and then making
them cry.

The Club believes that there is already a
programme like this on television, but that is only to
be expected, as we do not do original ideas.

We did have an original idea once — in 1978, we
think it was — for a portable device consisting of a
circular piece of fabric on spokes radiating from the
top of a carrying stick to protect people from the rain
but, alas, it proved to be not in the least original at
all. We gave up on original ideas after that.

Anyway, our own programme in this genre will be
called, we think, *The XXL Factor*, but just to keep it in

the tradition of such programmes our presenter,
Jean, will host it in the manner of a stringy-haired,
puckered-face old boot who will fold her arms
contemptuously while shouting: 'ARE YOU
STUPID? HOW THICK CAN YOU GET? DO
YOU WANT TO GO TO AN EARLY GRAVE?
DO YOU? YOU DISGUST ME. YOU
SHOULD BE ASHAMED OF YOURSELF. I
BET YOU FART BIG TIME!'

Now, you may also ask what qualifies Jean (from our
Worthing branch) to go around telling people they are
useless and pathetic lumps of lard? At this point, she
would have to stop you as she *is* a doctor of nutrition
and a *proper* doctor of nutrition. She did not acquire a
meaningless PhD via a distance course from an
unaccredited American college, but got hers from the
fish shop. 'I'll have a nice bit of plaice and a doctorate,
please,' she said to the fishmonger. 'Certainly,
madam,' said the fishmonger. 'I've got some lovely
doctorates. Fresh in this morning.' In the end, she
bought two, one for herself and one for her cat,
Tibbles, who will be helping out when she is either
away or has to lie down after lunch for several hours.
Tibbles is very excited as he has quite a dull life and is
looking forward to emptying people's food cupboards
and treating them as child murderers just because
there is a Kit-Kat in there and maybe a pear drop.

Anyway, Dr Jean's clinic, is now up and running and she has already begun seeing patients and responding to queries. Here are some typical examples:

Dear Doctor Jean

Yesterday, I gave my three children a packet of crisps each. Should I feel guilty?

Crisps! Crisps! Why don't you just push them in front of an oncoming train? Why don't you just get them to take a toaster into the bath? Crisps! Crisps! You should be ashamed of yourself. You're not fit to be a mother. You're heading towards an early grave. You make me sick. Guilty? People have got life for less than this.

Dear Doctor Jean

I wonder if you could settle something of a quarrel between my wife and me. My wife is not a fan of yours particularly and even said the other day. 'What does she think her own doings smell of? Pot-pourri?' I, on the other hand, am a big fan of yours and suspect they probably do. Am I right?

Naturally. Mine not only smell of pot-pourri but are much in demand for the entrance halls of stately homes and similar, or would be if only the National Trust had been more open-minded and did not respond to my offer with, 'We must decline at this time and for all time, as everybody's doings stink, even yours. Get over it, you stringy old witch, and do not bother us again.' Alas, I had a similar response from both English Heritage and the Ritz hotel chain. Anyone would think that I did not have a doctorate from a fully unaccredited fishmonger or hadn't spent years doing no research whatsoever.

Dear Doctor Jean
The more fruit and veg I eat, the more I yearn for a Pot Noodle. I do give in occasionally, I admit. Is this normal?
Look, the odd Pot Noodle isn't going to do you any harm. Oh dear, sorry, I went out of character there for a minute. Let's start again: Pot Noodle! Pot Noodle! Are you mad? Are you insane? Do you want to go to an early grave? Do you have *any* idea what a Pot Noodle does to your insides? A Pot Noodle will not only clog up your arteries, it will also make your liver explode and force your kidneys up out of your ears. Do you get tummy aches? I knew it. It's your kidneys, forcing themselves upwards. Even the sniff of a Pot Noodle can paralyse you from the neck down. Did you know that? You're killing yourself. You're heading to an early grave. You are also at an increased risk of breast cancer, stroke, diabetes, moths in all your wardrobes and misplacing your keys. Your choice, fatso. Up to you, gut-bucket and pitiful

excuse for a human being. Why aren't you weeping with self-hate and shame yet? Do you think I've got all day?

Dear Doctor Jean

I tried your Chinese mushroom, Tibetan fingleberry and Venezuelan yongy-yongi fruit smoothie the other morning for breakfast and guess what? It made me sick! I was pretty miffed as it took me eight years and God knows what in travel costs to personally collect the ingredients. I even sprinkled the smoothie with the blue-green algae collected by big-breasted women at first tide during a full moon, as you suggested. I wish, now, that I'd just had a bowl of Special K! Help!

Oh, go away. I don't have the time for this. Tibbles and I have some more disgusting and impossible smoothie recipes to devise before setting up a website selling unproven nonsense to a gullible public. So shove off.

Dear Doctor Jean

I am a Nobel prize-winning physicist, a concert pianist, an Olympic swimmer, a world champion ice-dancer, a tireless charity worker and an exemplary spouse, parent and pet owner. However, I do have a weakness for chips. Can I feel proud of myself in any way whatsoever?

I am horrified at the way you live your life. What are you playing at? Such accomplishments count for nothing considering you are on your way to an early grave. Idiot!

Dear Doctor Jean

Last time I attended your clinic I was seen by a cat. Is this right and proper?

Yes. Dr Tibbles also has a doctorate and is no less qualified than I am.

Dear Doctor

Isn't everything in moderation the key?

No. For example, you must buy all my books in very, very large amounts. (P.S. Do you want to go to an early grave?)

We of the NDGC (GB) think Jean has done a terrific job. Well done, Jean!

The Not Smoking?

'Getting there, getting there. Can't think of anything else apart from: all the male presenters on the *Antiques Road Show* who look like they've had their hair styled over a cushion, the big poufs; cats who sit on the newspaper while you are trying to read it; pedestrians on zebra crossings who mouth "thank you" so now you have to wind the window down and shout, "Don't thank me, I only stopped because it is the law, love"; Gillian McKeith; someone eating the one thing in the fridge you've got your eye on, and might even be living for; Quick Ticket ticket machines that won't take your note however you angle the Queen's head and as it is always quicker joining the regular queue, what is the point?; apples with individual stickers on; all this rage, rage, rage; having nothing to look forward to or live for unless you count inspirational feminine hygiene products that are works of pure genius . . .'

Inspirational Feminine Hygiene Produc
that are Works of Pure Genius

What woman hasn't yearned to menstruate quietly? And now the Club has noticed that she can with the new Kotex 'Ultra Quiet . . . Shhh'. You may have noted it in Boots and thought, as we did, hurrah, an alternative to the noisy sanitary pad which, as we all know, is the most tiresome of feminine hygiene products, talking over *EastEnders* and running up the phone bill and always shouting, 'Hey, you up there, you may well complain about cramps and bloat and the ache in the small of your back but, let me tell you, it is certainly no party down here. Now, put on *Emmerdale* and pass the crisps while you're about it.' A noisy sanitary pad, as every woman knows, can also be very bossy and demanding. (It may, for example, always insist on Kettle Chips rather than the cheaper crisps, which is both expensive and trying.)

But a quiet sanitary pad, now there's a thing, and

just what all women have been waiting for all these years. Who hasn't said to themselves at some point, 'Oh, how I wish they'd invent a quieter sanitary pad.' And now here it is, with its 'unique design' guaranteeing 'the ultimate in discretion'. The *ultimate* in discretion? Is this not a dream come true? Most of us would have settled for 'the first step in a distinctly discreet direction', but the ultimate? They spoil us, those Kotex people, they really do.

The 'unique design'? This turns out to be a pouch of cloth-like material that does not rustle or crackle or make any of the usual tell-tale sounds that indicate you might be doing something in the toilet that probably has nothing to do with eating Quality Street or making handmade greeting cards with tissue-paper roses and cellophane bows. The silent sanitary pad will, of course, prove particularly useful in public conveniences where, it goes without saying, you have no wish to broadcast your menstrual state to other users, all of whom will be women who also menstruate every month, have done so since they were 12 and will continue to do so until they are 50 or thereabouts. So . . . shhhh!

Truly, if you didn't know that a certain Kimberley Clark was in charge of Kotex, you'd think that these pads must have been invented by a man. Men fear women and their periods a great deal, possibly even more than they fear misplacing the remote control or being put in sole charge of a small person called 'Your Child'. We don't know why men find it all so awful, but they do. I suppose most women were initially desensitised by our mothers who, as they approached puberty, would say something comforting along the lines of, 'Darling, something wonderful and beautiful is shortly going to happen to your body and it's nothing to be scared about and it's called THE CURSE, HA, HA, HA!'

But men can't deal with it at all. Should you work in an office where all the bosses are male and say something along the lines of, 'Look, I've just been diagnosed with terminal cancer and my leg has fallen off as well as my elbows, can I go home this afternoon?' they will say, 'No. Sorry. Just can't spare you.' But if you were to say, 'I've got women's troubles . . .' the response will be, 'Go. Go. Take the rest of the day off. Take the week off, the month, the year. On full pay. On extra pay. Take whatever it takes but just do not, we beg you, go into any details. SHHH!'

Naturally, it would be rather different if men menstruated, as they'd transform it into a boastful event, and would probably sit around all day discussing how big and how long. 'I went for nine days with no let up last month,' one will say. 'Nine days with no let up?' the other will say. 'That's nothing. I once went for a full fortnight and it was so heavy I never got off the Ultra Super Duper Maxis with the Boeing 747 Wings.' There would be no 'shhh' about it. Their sanitary pads – Kotex Ultra Loud . . . Bang! – would go off like firecrackers.

Still, it's always good to have more choice, particularly as the sanitary pads currently on offer only include Mini, Regular, Maxi, Everyday, Every Other Day, Incredibly Thin, Incredibly Fat, Super, Super Plus, Overnight, Teatime, Elevenses, Long, Super Long, Extra Super Long – which can also be tied between two trees for a most absorbent and attractive summertime hammock. And wings. Big wings, medium wings, little wings, all of which will somehow end up gluing themselves to your inner thigh, so giving you an inadvertent Brazilian when it comes to removal. If the rustle doesn't give you away, then the 'ouch, ow, eek' certainly might. Also, if you opt for a winged one, try not to mistake it, when rummaging in the depths of your handbag, for your new funky flip phone, as you will end up with a pad stuck to the side of your head. It's an unfortunate look, by all accounts, not that it has ever happened to any of us. Or maybe it has. We're not saying . . . Shhh!

The Not Smoking?

'It's now only: pedestrians on zebra¶ crossings who
are so slow that no wonder you have to rev your
engine at them; buying the wrong kind of double
cream and whipping it for days to no effect; letters
from the council saying your overgrown front hedge
represents a danger to blind people; those who say
they are going to give something "110 per cent", the
idiots; blind pedestrians who fall into your hedge
leaving unsightly, blind-pedestrian-shaped holes; all
pedestrians, basically; plums that won't ripen and
then go off; the staff in JJB Sports who appear to have
graduated from the London School of Dunno. ('Why
are these trainers twice the price of those?' 'Dunno.'
'Do you have a pulse?' 'Dunno.' 'How about I stab
you through the heart to find out? Would that be
OK?' 'Dunno'); peaches that won't ripen and then
go off; supermarket packers who put the potatoes on
top of the eggs, the ignorant twits; all soft fruit
because soft fruits are bastards; anyone who does yoga
and meditates even though we all know it's just sitting
around doing nothing dressed up as a search for
spiritual fulfilment . . .'

How Do You Find Spiritual Fulfilment?

We are grateful to the author of this book – as well as a founder of the NDGC (Golders Green branch) – for giving us the following talk on her own particular search:

'Ladies, spiritual fulfilment is what we are all searching for, one way or another. Maybe there have been times when you've thought you have found it. Indeed, I thought I'd found it once when, after 14 hours of rummaging in TK Maxx, I came upon a Vivienne Westwood handbag for £17.99. I felt very, very good about that, ladies, but I'm not entirely convinced it counts. Further, a day or so later, I realised that while it was a Vivienne Westwood handbag, and while it was £17.99, it was very pink and really most unpleasant, which is probably why no one else had snapped it up. All I am saying is that in the search for spiritual fulfilment, you may find that TK

Maxx can turn out to be very disappointing. I can't speak for Matalan, but have my suspicions. I did once try yoga, but it was silly and banal and the Lycra went up my bottom. I have also tried aromatherapy, but I got a shoe and a Cornish pasty thrown at me.

'So, why not Kabbalah, ladies? It is all the rage, after all. Madonna is really into it, as are Demi Moore, Ashton Kutcher, Sandra Bernhardt, Guy Ritchie and John Gray, who wrote *Men are from Mars, Women are from Venus* and many, many permutations thereafter: *Mars and Venus on a Date*; *Mars and Venus Diet and Exercise Solution*; *Mars and Venus in the Bedroom*; *Mars and Venus Starting Over*; *Mars and Venus, 365 Ways to Keep Your Love Alive* but not, alas, *Venus Says: Look, Don't Disappear into Your Cave Every Time I Mention a Light Bulb Needs Changing. Do You Have Any Idea How Irritating It is? Get out, Get out, and Get out Now!*

'Maybe Kabbalah is not for you, but I did think it might be for me. I am a Jew, after all, although something of a mixed-up Jew as I don't do any Jewish things, so often wonder if I have any proper right to call myself one. My son, whose father is not Jewish, might be even more confused. "Mum," he once asked when he was little, "as you're Jewish, am I Jewish?" "Yes, darling," I said, "at least according to the Jewish religion you are." "So has my penis been criticised, then?" he asked. "No, darling," I said. "Will I have to get it criticised when I'm older?" he asked. "I expect so," I said. "Your father certainly did, still does, quite a lot." "Does it hurt, Dad?" "You bet," said his father, who does not take criticism well, always taking it extremely personally. Sometimes, he can disappear into his cave for so long, ladies, I stop setting the table for him. Sometimes it's hard to be a Venusian, don't you think?

'So, Kabbalah: all the rage. It's a strange thing, because Jews have never wanted to attract non-Jews, have never, ever been evangelical. Indeed, when your doorbell goes and you are not expecting anybody, you may think, "Oh no, Jehovah's." You may think, "Oh no, Mormons." You may think, "Oh no, Seventh Day Adventists." You may think: "Oh no, Sixth Day Adventists, a day early." You may think, "Oh no, NPower." But you don't think, "Oh no, a Jew, come to convert me. Be off, Jew, be off, and I don't care how much it will reduce my bills. I'm quite happy with British Gas." You do not then have to get the man about the house to turf them out, which is good, because the man is still in the cave, which is a pain, as there is still that light bulb that needs changing. When you give a man unsolicited advice, John Gray says, do you know how unloving you sound? Yes, John. I think we bloody do. In turn, do you know what it is like to be a Venusian, always bumping into things in the dark?

'However, this said, I'm not sure that the current Kabbalah has a great deal in common with the original Kabbalah, the Jewish mystical tradition based on the book of Zohar, written in the second century and so complex that, traditionally, it was reserved for the most learned and pious. Indeed, orthodox Jews are not even allowed to study Kabbalah – effectively the "soul" of the Torah – until they are 40. They would argue, I'm guessing, that the sort of Kabbalah endorsed by the likes of Madonna and Demi and so on is a grotesque, New Age distortion brought about by profiteers offering simple, self-help-style answers to complex questions for cash.

'I once tried to be a profiteer offering simple answers to complex questions for cash but, ladies, I wasn't very good at it. "Why are we here?" people would ask. "Cheese," I would say. "That's £27.50 plus VAT." "What I'm asking is: what is the meaning of life?" they would persist. "Cheese," I would say, "and as I've told you twice it's now £65.99 plus VAT. Now get out my face." Strangely, I had a lot of trouble getting people to pay up and failed to make any profit whatsoever.

'As it is, you can get Kabbalah essentials, those little bits of red thread to wear around the wrist, from any haberdashery counter for next to nothing, which is, surely, a scandal considering you can also get one from www.kabbalah.com for $26.00. So I have bought a book, *The Power of Kabbalah*, by Yehuda Berg, which comes endorsed by Madonna ('The ideas in this book are earth-shattering and yet so simple') and John Gray ('This book provides a simple yet powerful and profound message for both novices and seasoned seekers alike'). The book itself makes no claims for itself beyond 'This book contains the secrets of the universe and the meaning of our lives'. What? It's not cheese? Anyway, in my pursuit of spiritual fulfilment and enlightenment, I intend to study it closely, but like the look of it already, as there is a chapter called 'The Power of Light'. Light, light. Wouldn't that be nice?

'(Have since studied it closely by reading the first two pages. It's crap. I'm off to Matalan.)'

We thanked this very fine person for her talk, even though it failed to be illuminating in any way whatsoever. She then agreed to give us a talk on the 'work—life balance', which none of us asked for, but there you have it.

What about Your Work–Life Balance?

Who doesn't worry about their work–life balance? And who isn't pleased that the whole work–life balance business is finally getting proper attention at last? It is an extremely important thing to hang on to. Indeed, just the other week, ladies, I lost my work–life balance in Waitrose and had to hold on to a chiller cabinet to steady myself. 'Are you OK?' asked another shopper. 'Can I get you anything?' I said no thanks, that I'd just lost my work–life balance for a moment, but was already feeling less giddy. I hate to think what would happen if, say, I lost my work–life balance at the wheel of a car. It doesn't bear thinking about. As it is, a friend of mine lost hers at the top of the stairs one day, tumbled, and ended up in A&E. The doctors were not, apparently, that sympathetic. 'If you only stopped fretting about this work—life nonsense,' they said, 'and just got on with it, muddling through as people have done for generations, you wouldn't have this trouble.' My friend was horrified at being treated like a neurotic ninny with a self-indulgent malady, and is now complaining through the relevant channels. As she says, until the medical profession takes work—life imbalances seriously there'll be many more horrible accidents such as hers.

It's hard to tell where this work-life business comes from exactly, but it appears to come wrapped in what is now called the 'Science of Happiness', a serious enterprise that has led to books, TV shows, Professors of Happiness and even an academic periodical, the *Journal of Happiness Studies*. Certainly, happiness as a science is something everyone should take most seriously, as I do. I'm even hoping that one day I'll be awarded a Chair of Happiness at a major university, and that I will not only be allowed to choose the Chair — an Eames lounger would make me happy, I think — but will also be able to lounge on it whenever I fancy, not just when my work—life balance is disturbed and

I need a sit-down. I may even be allowed to lounge on it while fondling an expensive handbag, which would be perfect happiness. Indeed, little makes a woman happier than fingering an expensive handbag while lounging on her Chair of Happiness, unless it is finding herself in the same room as someone fatter than her. This is shameful, shallow and disgusting, but such a happy event all the same. In fact, after a lifetime of reading *Cosmo* and *Vogue*, and now *Heat* and *Grazia*, I would add that, for much of the Western world, the following highly scientific formula covers it when it comes to happiness.

Being Thin + Buying Lots of Stuff = Happiness

Yes, this has been tested on animals but, as sending a very thin mouse into Harvey Nichols with a limitless credit card proved, animals and humans are too different in this instance for the resultant data to be useful. It didn't buy a thing. It didn't even seem interested, even though the scientists kept entreating it, 'Go on, treat yourself!' The mouse, I should add, wasn't harmed in any way, and wasn't forced to try on bikinis. Not in front of a three-way mirror, anyway, as that's cruel (although they did it to rabbits well into the 1970s). As scientists now know, and everyone else knew anyway:

Bikini + Three-Way Mirror =
Complete Abject Misery

Further:

$$\text{Bikini} + \text{Three-Way Mirror} + \text{Cellulite}$$
$$= \text{Strong Suicidal Feelings}^*$$

Obviously, as the Science of Happiness is a new discipline, more work is needed, which may or may not be done, depending on the work–life balance: anyone may have to race home at any time to lob a baby about. By the way, if you feel your work–life balance going, breathing into a paper bag helps. This much, at least, is known.

Dare We Ask?

'Oh, I'm definitely over the worst. Nothing bothers me now, unless you count: the phone going and it's a PR asking if I'm planning any major features on Appletise this week; the phone going and it's a so-called friend who is a smoker and proceeds to inhale and exhale with obscene gusto; the phone going and it's a young niece who wants to play "guess the noise", so you run a tap while she does "flicking a shoelace against the washing machine" and then complains when you don't get it; the phone going at all; the cost of replacing phones once you have torn them from

---

* Even the rabbits said as much.

the wall and tried to smoke them; power-chewing
Nicorette until you get nauseous and then vomit;
partners who say it is easy to give up smoking, I did it!
– even though they have only ever smoked half a one
at a party in 1977; the Nicorette instruction booklet
that tells you to take up a new hobby (could it be
homicide?); the new phone going and it's your niece
wondering why you can't get "breathing on a
wastepaper basket"; healthy, fit people who are
spiritually fulfilled (what bores); and basically anyone
and everyone wherever they are and whatever they are
doing because I hate them and wish they were dead
just as they wish I was dead.'

You Could Just Start Smoking Again

'Um . . . OK.'

5

Fashion and Beauty

Just like parenting experts, the advice of fashion experts shifts hourly, and sometimes even half-hourly, and then, to top it all, they land you with the 'sexy sweater dress' which, after the one sit-down, retains the shape of your bottom, so making you look like about as sexy as a badly knitted baboon. However, this doesn't mean you should ever underplay the importance of what you wear. Indeed, as Trinny and Susannah always put it, more or less: 'Poor Mary. Her marriage has failed. Her business has gone bust. Her house has been repossessed. Her kids are on crack. Her legs have dropped off. Her head is on the wrong way round. Her cakes never rise. Sooze, what she really, really needs in her life at this point is a little shrug cardigan from Next. Let's go!' Anyway – here we present the real, real facts.

Accessories: The right bag, shoes, jewellery or
sunglasses truly *can* make an outfit, just as the wrong
accessories can ruin one. One of our Club members
discovered this to her own cost just the other day
when she set out for Budgens having accessorised her
outfit with chest waders, snorkel and a little Hitler-
style moustache and it proved a big, big mistake. As
she says: 'These accessories not only ruined the line
of my dress – utterly – but also, once the snorkel
misted up, I kept bumping into things and
ricocheting off the cheese counter and this so
unsettled my moustache it somehow ended up above
my left eyebrow. I was then escorted from the
building by two uniformed chaps who practically
threw me out on to the pavement with a "And don't
wade back in here ever again!" "Damn," I thought. "I
must have worn the wrong accessories!"' We urge you
not to make the same mistake.

Top Five Items to Avoid: (1) the sweater dress,
obviously; (2) the wrap-around skirt that will unwrap
wherever it so fancies; (3) the strapless bra which will
steadily work its way down to your waist; (4) the tiny
thong that will bisect your bum like a cheese slicer;
(5) yesterday's sock caught up a trouser leg. Also
beware the multi-layered 'Boho' look which can make
you look like you've had a run in with the washing

line. The look is said to be Sienna Miller meets
Virginia Woolf, which might not have been that
interesting a meeting:

SIENNA: 'Shall we go down Accessorize for yet more
African-inspired beaded cummerbunds?'
VIRGINIA: 'Yeah, alright then.'

The Benetton Trap: Oh, yes, Benetton is a very, very
clever shop where beautifully folded sweaters in lovely
colour gradations — so reminding you of all the happy
hours you spent arranging and rearranging your
Caran d'Ache colouring pencils a child — somehow
lead you to conclude it would be really fun to own a
lemon cardigan. It is not, never has been and never
will be fun to own a lemon cardigan. It's a trap. When
you get home you will think, 'Bloody hell, what do I
want a lemon-coloured cardigan for?' Your family
will say, 'Bloody hell, what do you want a lemon-
coloured cardigan for?' You friends will say, 'A
lemon-coloured cardigan, how crap is that?' Late one
night you will find yourself sitting up in bed, crying
and scissoring it to bits. You can't take it back because
if you do you will be seduced all over again, and will
return with three lime-coloured jumpers, two baby-
blue ones and a tank-top in tangerine.

That Shoe Thing: If a shoe exists, buy it. If you don't, you will regret it for ever. On your deathbed, you will be thinking, 'I wish I had bought those shoes.' This would be a shame, as there are so many other things you could be thinking, like, 'I wish I'd bought more crap, generally,' and, 'I wish I'd spent more time in the office because then I'd have been a lot more successful as well as more up on the gossip.'

What Not to Wear (For Sure): So as not to give the impression you have given up on fashion entirely, although who would blame you, it might be wise to steer clear of: big zippered fleeces; anything from Cotton Traders; trousers hoiked up high (surely it's only a matter of time before Patrick Moore and Ian Paisley choke on their own waistbands); anything with an elasticated or tie waist even though it will be really, really comfy, damn it; and sweatshirts decorated with appliqué horses or circus animals, particularly seals balancing balls on their noses. You should not include bum bags because, whatever anyone says, they are very handy for keeping your keys and coins in and are sometimes even double-zippered for this very purpose. However, they are called 'fanny packs' in America and we would strongly advise against these, as last time a member packed her fanny she couldn't get the creases out for ages. Not even with the iron on 'steam'.

Shopping: Always go shopping on your own. Ditch friends either for the afternoon, or generally. (Friends can be tiresomely selfish, going on and on about their problems as if you don't have enough of your own.) Certainly, never ever go shopping with a pre-teen or teenage girl. Everything you show them will be 'yukky'. To save time, it may be advisable to stick your head round the door of shops and shout, 'Hey, anything in here that's not yukky?' There won't be anything that isn't yukky, as there never is, but at least you'll have been spared having to go though clothes rack after clothes rack as she recites: 'Yukky. Yukky. Really yukky. Yukky. Yukky. Hang on, this is . . .' What, what, WHAT? '. . . yukky.' It would be wholly irresponsible to turn her round on the same spot 79 times and then 'accidentally' lose her somewhere on Oxford Street when she's only 10 and your niece from the sticks. But all the same.

The Flesh Factor: Never show too much flesh. If you're revealing lots of cleavage, for example, have you legs hidden — and vice versa. Don't let it all hang out. It's sexier to leave a little to the imagination, although some people find it hard to imagine a

scorched fanny, which is why we've posted the
photographs at ww.packyourfannyatyourperil.com as
a warning to all that, in these circumstances, never set
the iron to higher than 'viscose and other synthetics'.
Lastly, if Next don't have a little shrug cardigan to
make Mary feel whole again, there is every chance
Principles will. 'Let's go, Trin, let's go!'

No, Let's Go to Bodenland!

Ah, Bodenland. If you have ever ordered a Boden catalogue, or have visited the Boden website and have somehow registered, you will receive regular emails from Johnnie Boden. He may write: 'A Great Big Hello! I'm Johnnie Boden and I'd like to thank you for visiting my website . . . I set out to provide competitively priced clothing that doesn't date . . . I wanted to do this with a sense of fun . . . You may not want to take my word for it (as I can go on a bit), so just put us to the test . . .'

Possibly you have never responded, which is terribly bad-mannered, so we suggest you get your act together and reply. You may like to adapt the following example:

AND A GREAT BIG HELLO TO YOU, TOO, JOHNNIE! But I'm going to go one better by offering you A GREAT BIG VELVET-TRIMMED HELLO IN SASSY JEANS AND A PRETTY PEARL CARDIE! I do love your catalogue, Johnnie. Absolute bliss. I love all the pretty ladies with cute wrinkled noses, hair scrunched in makeshift chignons, and their names always followed by parentheses to tell you something whimsical about them: Caroline (favourite word: jammy); Natalia (style icon: Kate Moss). Cute.

My name, Johnnie, is Deborah Ross (style icon: Olive from *On the Buses*; ask anybody) and I would like to thank you for thanking me for once visiting your website. I do visit your website every now and then but have never actually purchased anything, which is weird, as more than anything I yearn to live in Bodenland, where the children frolic in puddles in their floral wellies and the women have all the time in the world to drape themselves fetchingly on driftwood.

Oh please, Johnnie, let me live in Bodenland. I could drape fetchingly on driftwood, given half the chance, and I've never managed a chignon that wasn't makeshift, although there is makeshift and makeshift, and I promise you I can take makeshift to levels your models don't even get near. You might not take my word for it, as I can go on a bit, but you really should. Ask anybody. They may add that some days my hair looks like an exploding gorse bush but that's only because they can't recognise a makeshift chignon when they see one, Johnnie. That's what that is about.

Also, Johnnie, I promise not to bring my partner (pet hate: me; secret desire: a pretty homemaker with a cute wrinkled nose) to Bodenland. He would let us all down badly, Johnnie. He is not called Simon or Richard and, get this, Johnnie, he actually wears the stuff his mother buys him from the Blue Harbour range at Marks, which demonstrates what a non-aspirational loser he is. It pains me to say this, but I'll say it all the same: he is the sort of man who wouldn't recognise moleskin if the poor mole was skinned right under his nose. See what I have to live with, Johnnie?

Actually, we don't do too badly here in Crouch End. As it happens, there is always quite a lot of Flippy Retro Linen Skirt action going on down the Broadway, which makes for a gentle breeze, and so many small girls in your Fab ice-lolly swimsuits down Park Road Pool that I sometimes think if I see another one I'll have to bite her armbands when no one is looking, or even when someone is looking, what the hell.

Only joking, Johnnie! I just wanted you to
know that I, too, have a great sense of fun. I simply
adore the mini-Bodens with their treehouses
and ponies and whose aspirations are cutely
parenthesised, like Freya (6, architect) and Ludo
(4, stockbroker). Wouldn't it be awful if they grew
up to be Asboed binge-drinkers and crack fiends,
although I'd like to see their parents' faces all
the same.

However, Crouch End still has a long way to go,
as our Broadway is hardly a sun-dappled
boardwalk, and we don't even have any misty fields
through which we can all swish in long velvety skirts
while taking a break from leaning against the Aga
in sassy stretch bootlegs. We have the car park
behind Budgens, but it is far from ideal. I'm not
sure an electric hob cuts it either.

Now, Johnnie, I have always desperately wished
to ask you something: where is that Bodenland
beach? It's not a beach I've ever been to, but I
would so like to. It's a beach where the sun always
shines while mini-Bodens companionably
rockpool or jump from jetties and actually keep
their sunhats *on*. It's a place where no sand ever gets
into the sandwiches and wasps don't attack and
squabbling siblings don't beat the hell out of each
other and entire families who hate each other

don't end up shivering behind windbreaks and pointing at the sky, saying, 'it'll brighten up this afternoon.' Of course, there is no chance it will brighten up, ever, but you have to think so, or you might choose to end it all, don't you think, Johnnie?

I'm guessing the Bodenland beach is not at Shoeburyness. Last time I went on a day trip to Shoeburyness, Johnnie, I saw a little boy hit his sister with a spade, which she would have taken well if she hadn't retaliated by kicking him in the balls and hollering, 'That'll teach ya, shit face.' I don't think it was Freya and Ludo. To hazard a guess, I'd say it might have been Blaine (6, hoodie) and Kayleigh (8, scratch-card addict). I would have had a word with their mum, but she was un-chignoned and micro-skirted and quite big — had obviously let herself go. She might even have been — look away here, Johnnie — a single mum with a job! I don't know what you do about people like that, Johnnie. Where do you start in teaching them that there is a world of difference between sassy and tarty? And how are you going to hang on to a nice breadwinning man called Simon if you can't differentiate between the two?

Perhaps, Johnnie, you'll let me know ASAP if I can come to Bodenland? I'll try not to sneak in my shell suit (candy-pink), fond of it as I am. I'm makeshifting a chignon even as I write.

Yours

Deborah Ross
(favourite words: keep that bloody sunhat on or it's a slap for you, young lady).

Beauty

Beauty is only skin deep, which is a great shame if, say, you have ravishing kidneys and the most divine thyroid gland. 'My kidneys are ravishing and my thyroid gland is simply divine,' you may tell those people at Storm or Elite or Models One, but will they care? No, they will not. Although everyone says it is what is inside that truly counts, what is outside truly counts for a lot, lot more, if it isn't everything. How to attain that skin-deep beauty, though? Simple. Creams, creams and more creams — blow the budget! — but if you don't want to end up disappointed, and feeling as if you've wasted your money, you may wish to try the Non-Domestic Goddess Club's own range, Oil of Cliché. It is very, very good and actually does everything it says it will.

At Long Last, a Skincare Range that Does Everything It Says It Will

Everywhere you turn now it is anti-ageing this and anti-ageing that, so you might very well be interested in the NDGC's rather different, age-accepting range, Oil of Cliché. It has been especially developed for all those women who have fully tried to love the skin they're in, looked at it from all angles, and thought, nope, no can do, you're having a laugh, the cellulite on that alone would make four Keira Knightleys, two Kate Winslets and a size 16 puffa coat (full length). As for the pores, you could lose a boot in any one of them. We know, there is this thinking that if you keep after nature determinedly and doggedly enough you will attain the upper hand, but let us tell you something about nature: she's a bitch. No matter what you do, what you spend, nature is going to pelt you with those signs of ageing: lines and wrinkles; uneven skin tone and pores to lose boots in. You may even wake up one day and find that your pores have actually swallowed your face.

Now, Oil of Cliché, which has been developed by the NDGC's extremely scientific scientists who aren't just grey-haired actors in white coats, whatever anyone might say, contains secret, patented ingredients that would, of course, knock your little socks off if only you knew what they were.* It's also been clinically proven in a clinic by people who go about clinically proving these things, or would have been if we hadn't got lost on the way, but it's good and greasy all the same. However, what makes the Oil of Cliché range so special is that it absolutely guarantees to make no difference whatsoever. This means you pay the sort of money you would otherwise spend on such creams, but aren't disappointed when they don't work. In fact, we can honestly say we've yet to have a single disappointed customer! That is: 100 per cent of the women we would have tested it on had we not got lost on the way to the clinic said it made absolutely no difference to them, even though they were willing to pretend it had, just to justify the expense to themselves!

Indeed, just a few weeks ago we sold a pot of our Age Happens, That's Life, Get Over It serum to a lady who, when she returned recently for a new supply (false bottom; didn't last two minutes), well, we just couldn't get over the lack of difference in her. 'Madam,' we gasped, 'you look almost exactly the same as last time we saw you. See, this product

* They include ground ants' knees and the juice from a full kilo of Werther's Originals, but we are not saying more than that, as the other ingredients are very secret and very patented.

actually fulfils its promises!' She said it was the first time she had ever bought an expensive beauty product and not felt grotesquely cheated in some way, or that she had failed it by not being diligent or dogged enough because that's how you are made to feel, after all. We said, 'Madam, if you don't come back in 10 years looking 10 years older we will eat our hats.' We don't wear hats, as it happens, but we do wear those white coats that make us look all doctorly even though we spent only half a day training at some beauty school off Bond Street. We love our coats. It makes us feel so much less like just another shop worker. At Oil of Cliché we are not only trained to say all the usual things — 'Madam, that lipstick really suits you!' — but also, 'Madam, the chances of you reversing the signs of ageing are actually up there with you ever reversing a tank up your arse, so you might as well buy this as anything else.' This is why we insist that all Oil of Cliché staff do half a day, instead of the usual quarter.

Anyway, that lady was so thrilled by the way Oil of Cliché didn't let her down that she purchased some other items from our range. Of course we sell special, intensive creams for all those bits you've never even thought of before; not just the eye area, but also the bridge of your nose and a cream for your left temple and a separate cream for your right temple as your left and right temples have different needs entirely, madam, oh yes, and we should know because we wear white coats and trained for half a day at a beauty school instead of the usual quarter. She said she would start with our Age-Accepting Non-Transforming Right-Temple Gel and if she found it made no difference whatsoever, she would return for the left. As this particular product comes in a tiny little jar with very thick walls and a false bottom that is practically at the top, we are fully expecting her back any minute now. And here she is. 'Madam, you still don't look any more youthful. Not a jot!' Oil of Cliché. Not just because you're worth it, but because you are going to get older anyway.

Yes, You are Going to Get Older Anyway

And is it any fun, being an older woman? Many older women complain. We are rarely noticed, are all but invisible, they will say. It's like we're not good for anything any more. We're made to feel as if we are just cluttering up the place. Oh, come on, girls. There are still many uses for you. For example:

Interiors: Older women can often be used to good effect around the home. An older woman, for example, can make an excellent floor lamp, although will obviously have to be nailed down. This is usually a two-person job: one to hold, one to hammer. However, if she is approaching crunch time in the egg department, she will not only glow nicely in a very energy-efficient way but will also give off enough heat to dry your socks on. Be warned, though, her temperature can zoom up and down quite unexpectedly. But if you wish she had a thermostat, how do you think she feels?

As for an older woman with a hump, do not use as a floor lamp because she can be put to better use as a bedside table. Two older women with humps can make a lovely pair of bedside tables. (See this month's *Elle Decoration* for a beautiful example, photographed in a house they say real people live in, but we don't know.) If you are a first-time homeowner on a budget, it's worth asking around to see if any friends or family have any unwanted older women knocking about. Ask them to check their attics and cellars and sheds and all the other places it is possible to abandon an older woman who, in an ideal world, would have disappeared quietly of her own accord, so allowing everyone else to get on with it. Generally, the renovation of older women is tricky, and possibly best left to the experts, but if you promise miraculous results by some absurd cream made from baby badger lard mixed, three to one, with parrot beak shavings collected only during a full moon, she will give you lots and lots and lots of money, no further questions asked, just hand it over.

Older women do not, by the way, like to be rag-rolled or stencilled. One thing you should know about women over 40 is that they remember the eighties and can clearly recall how awful it all was the first time round. Women over 40 can work well as antimacassars except on those occasions when they are cross.' On these occasions, a woman over 40 does not work well as an antimacassar as she may bite. You'll notice her then, and no mistake. You may wish to check, before sitting down, that the antimacassar isn't Esther Rantzen, because then you've had it, basically. You can thrash and thrash but you'll never throw her off. Better people than you have tried.

Exteriors: Women over 40 can be put to many uses outside: benches; bird-tables; patios; goal-posts; trellises; water features; hammocks; but not pebbledashing, as it looks silly. In fact, we know someone who pebbledashed their entire house in Patricia Hodge and it looked very silly indeed.

Older women do make an excellent mulch but, if there is any fight left in them, they may resist being composted or shredded. Do not attempt to force them into the compost bin/shredder if they have just applied one of their absurd creams, especially if it's more parts baby badger lard than parrots' beaks, as they'll be greasy as hell and shoot though your hands, whoosh, and over the fence and now look what you've done. You've landed your neighbour with a woman over 40. Great. What's he now meant to do with her? In short, it is best to wait it out until she has no fight left, which is only a matter of time, and she can then be composted or shredded without any problems. Dig the resultant mulch into your borders now and they'll come up lovely in July. One of our members dug some Pauline Quirke into her own borders last year and you've never seen such a display.

Kitchen: The meat of women over 40 is not much in demand, even though the Prince of Wales is a fan and would like to see it back on our dining tables. However, the bones can be used for stocks and soups. Boil for three to four hours with bay leaf, onion, black peppercorns and a couple of carrots. Strain, leave overnight, skim off fat, then add parsley and some finely shredded Sue Lawley and, *voilà*, there you have it. (If you have no Sue Lawley in the cupboard, you can use Vanessa Feltz, but you do not need as much. A little goes a long way.)

Transport: Older women have been successfully recycled as trams, trains and even cars. Indeed, one of our members drives around in a Vauxhall Corsa made from Anneka Rice and apparently it is a very fine little car, perfectly satisfactory in every way. People often wonder about what happened to Anneka Rice, and now you know. However, people don't wonder about older men because they are allowed to go on and on and on and on without remark. I should just say that the bendy bus made from Gloria Hunniford has not, thus far, proved a great success.

When It Comes Down to It, It is Just So Hard to be a Woman

For example, here are just a few of the things a woman has to do as summer approaches:

1) Apply self-tanning product so you don't frighten children with your winter-white luminosity.

2) Race round chemists in the hope of discovering a self-tan product remover so you don't frighten children with your terrifyingly EasyJet orange luminosity. ('What is that?' children will ask as you pass. 'That,' they will be told, 'is someone who did not properly exfoliate first, as always advised.')

3) Wax, shave, Veet and generally depilate like a loony while asking yourself, 'If I skip the bits I can't see, will I look like King Kong from behind?'

4) Apply polish to toes, badly. Remove and reapply. Badly. Repeat process long into the night, never getting anywhere.

5) Fret about what to wear to a summer wedding, which is obligatory, even if you haven't been invited to any.

6) Wax, shave, Veet and generally attempt to depilate the bits you can't see, as 27 people have already shouted out, 'Hey, King Kong' as they've come up behind you, and a dog even tried to have sex with the back of your leg.

7) Equip yourself with this season's funky high wedges and fall arse over tit at the entrance to Finsbury Park Tube station. 'Look like buggers, them shoes,' Jim, the *Big Issue* seller, will say, as if he is up on fashion (well, honestly).

8) Have another go at the toenails. Nope, still looks like a drunk with Parkinson's has been let loose on them.

9) Scoop up sleeveless tops in Gap/Zara/Mango/Topshop then promptly return on the grounds that the tone in your upper arms is shot.

10) Try not to cry in Gap/Zara/Mango/Topshop, even though the young sales assistants will snigger.

11) Pinch an inch and say you don't give a stuff even though you do.

12) Spend hours at www.figleaves.com searching for the perfect bikini which you'll never have the figure to wear.

13) Attend to hard skin on feet with a good pumicing unless it's so grim down there only a cheese-grater will do.

14) Try not to shout, 'YOU'LL ALL BE 40 ONE DAY!' at the sales assistants as you leave Gap/Zara/Mango/Topshop, because they simply won't believe it.

15) Search the internet for more realistic swimwear and luckily hit upon www.wholesomewear.com (so I think you'll know who we are on the beach).

16) Decide to give up on fake tans and go for the real thing. Drag out sun lounger from shed, bravely flick off spiders and desiccated moths with only the minimum amount of shrieking and whimpering, then lie down and get up (need sunglasses), lie down, get up (sun cream), lie down, get up (phone), lie down, get up (doorbell), lie down, leap up (spider in cleavage) and just generally go up, down, up, down, in, out, in, out, until you think, 'Oh, forget it.'

17) Pass the sign outside Fitness First that says 'Tone those wobbly bits for summer!' Backtrack and spit at it.
18) Fret about why you haven't been invited to any summer weddings, which is very annoying when you've put so much effort into thinking what you'd wear if you were.
19) Have another go at toenails . . . etc. etc.
20) You've even thought about the right hat.

And here's what men have to do:

1) Check if the big chef's hat and jokey barbecue apron will do for another year . . . Yup, just as funny.
2) Er . . . that's it.

So this is why the summer is womankind's burden, but still, it wouldn't do to take it out on men by letting them nibble at what they imagine are the last bits of cheese on the grater. Or would it?

6

The Male

It is now quite commonplace for women to more or less say, 'Men, what a shower.' They will then go on to rubbish them. They are useless, hopeless, unnecessary, annoying. They bite the cheese and then put it back in the fridge. They can't 'multi-task'. They have no idea who their children's teachers are. They sometimes have no idea who their own children are. 'Who is this small person eating Shreddies at the breakfast table this morning? Have we met?' They never stack or unstack the dishwasher, imagining what? That elves do it in the middle of the night? And so on and so on, proving what exactly? That women are superior in every way? That men would be lost without them? This is absurd. Indeed, there are many things which men can do well that women simply can't and what is the point in pretending otherwise? Come on, sisters, face it, men are superior in many, many respects. It goes against the current thinking but it's a fact all the same.

Men are Better at Many Things, and That's a Fact

Not yet convinced? Try the following for
size:

Have you ever met a woman who falls asleep in front
of the television at 9 p.m., wakes up at 2 a.m.,
stumbles off to bed, ricochets noisily off the
wardrobe, then scratches her private parts with gusto
before falling flat on her back, where she will spend
the rest of the night making a noise alternating
between an oncoming train and a peculiar nasal
whinnying? Sisters, let us be entirely honest, men are
good at this and we are not.

Have you ever met a woman who refuses to call a
plumber when the pipe behind the washing machine
develops a leak and instead keeps insisting, 'I'll fix it,
I'll fix it,' although when she does get round to it,

several months later, bumbles around so clumsily she causes a second leak but still will not call a plumber and still keeps insisting, 'I can fix it,' while looking daggers at you, you great big nag. Sisters, let us be entirely honest, men are good at this and we are not.

Have you ever met a woman who buys a pair of £8 cords from George at Asda and then doesn't wear them in case they are a 'fashion mistake' and have to be returned? Sisters, let us be entirely honest, men are good at this and we are not.

Have you ever met a woman who, when driving, has punched her navigator full in the face for simply reading the map upside down and so now we are miles from anywhere, and going to be really late, so well done you, hope you're proud of yourself? Sisters, let us be entirely honest, men are good at this and we are not.

Have you ever met a woman who falls asleep in front of the television at 9 p.m., opens her eyes briefly at 10ish, says, 'I don't know what you see in *Sex in the City/Desperate Housewives/ER/Lost*', has a slight go at her privates — saving the real gusto for later: something to look forward to — then closes her eyes again, although perhaps not before a last, 'I can fix it, I can'? Sisters, let us be entirely honest, men are good at this and we are not.

Have you ever met a woman who will buy her elderly, infirm father a machine for stripping wallpaper for his 87th birthday on the grounds that 'B&Q was on my way home' and 'What do you mean try another shop . . . when I'd been to one already?' Sisters, let us be entirely honest, men are good at this and we are not.

Have you ever met a woman who, on passing the Gadget Shop, will declare that the little remote control car is the best thing ever and I must get one and while I'm in there I think I'll also get one of those little robots that serve cocktails as you just can't beat a little robot that serves cocktails? Sisters, let us be entirely honest, men are good at this and we are not.

Have you ever met a woman who has a secret 'short-cut' that is actually longer than the long-cut but who will persist in proudly calling it 'my short-cut' even though all stopwatches and odometers — and even the use of two cars to see who gets home first — prove otherwise, every single time, none of which count 'because I got caught behind a milk float'? Sisters, let us be entirely honest, men are good at this and we are not.

Have you ever met a woman who, on being told that a particular skin cream will make her skin appear illuminated, radiant and smoother over time as a more youthful appearance is simultaneously achieved, will write it off as the waste of money it is, refuse to buy it and walk away with both her dignity and her self-respect intact? Sisters, let us be entirely honest, men are good at this and we are so not.

Have you ever met a woman who, in spite of her astonishing ability to multi-task – and even multi-task while multi-tasking – canNOT keep up with the plot of a Mafia film – as in who has double-crossed whom – and so will, admittedly, annoy everybody by saying over and over, 'I don't understand who killed Frankie, or why'? Actually, there are many, many women who are like this. This, sisters, we are good at. You might even say we excel.

Battle of the Sexes: It's War Out There

The other evening I, personally, called an emergency meeting of the Non-Domestic Goddess Club of Great Britain, requesting that, as I had a very urgent matter to discuss, everyone should do their very best to attend unless they forgot, had something better to do or, at the last minute, just couldn't be bothered. No other excuses, I stressed, would be even remotely acceptable. It's important. There's a war going on and somehow, some way, we *have* to win it.

Well, the first to arrive was Mrs Butler, who asked, as you might, 'What war?'

'A battle-of-the-sexes-type war,' I replied, adding, 'one of those wars that begins with a niggle, escalates and can absolutely destroy a relationship or marriage.'

'By "niggle" in a marriage,' queried Mrs Butler,

'do you mean realising you hate each other and should never have got together in the first place, and wishing he was dead? Will there be tips on undetectable poisons and tampering with their car brakes?'

I said, 'Honestly, Mrs Butler, we did that last month. Didn't you attend?' She said not. She meant to, she said, but on that day her appendix burst and then her left leg fell off – 'In Sainsbury's, can you imagine? But they did carry it out to the car for me.'

I got a bit cross about this, I admit. 'Mrs Butler,' I said, 'unless you forgot, had something better to do or, at the last minute, simply could not be bothered, I don't want to hear it. I won't be fobbed off with such feeble reasons for not attending.'

She rejoined with, 'Oh, *and* I couldn't be bothered.' I said that was better. Thank you, Mrs Butler. Now that will be all. You may hop to your seat now.

I began the meeting. 'Ladies,' I said, 'this winter, what has preoccupied you for much of the time? Has it been baking?'

'No,' everyone cried.

'Has it been darning?'

'No,' everyone cried.

'Has it been getting the lawn mower blades sharpened in readiness for the spring?'

'Get a life!' everyone cried.

'Has it been leaving things at the bottom of the stairs to take up later and then never taking them?'

'Yes!' everyone cried.

OK, *apart* from leaving things at the bottom of the stairs to take up later but never taking them, have you also been engaged in . . . central heating wars?'

'Yes, yes, yes!' everyone cried.

I said, 'Ladies, if this war – and it is war, not a game – plays out in your homes anything like it does in mine, I'm guessing it goes like this, and always goes like this:

1) You, who feels the cold, turn the central heating on.
2) Your partner, who does not feel the cold, then turns it off.
3) You turn it back on.
4) He turns it back off.
5) On.
6) Off.
7) On.
8) Off.
9) On.
10) Off.

'And so on, until the very end of time itself. And is it any fun, ladies? Is it amusing in any way? No. Plus, if I'm guessing right, and I think I am, it can get dirty. Very dirty. On occasion, you may even meet at the thermostat while one is on-ing and the other is off-ing. This, of course, can result in a fist fight so, if you want my advice, always come prepared with, for example, a Dobermann and a bread knife. Alternatively, broken bottles, knuckle dusters and cricket bats are suitable.'

'Yippee!' exclaimed Mrs Butler. 'Good show!'

I pressed on. 'Further, you must be alert to cheating at all times. He may, for example, *not* turn the heating off after you have put it on, which you may think quite nice of him . . .'

'Does that mean we can't use the broken bottles, knuckle dusters or cricket bats . . .?' interrupted Mrs Butler.

'No,' I said, 'it does not, because what you will discover is that he has left the boiler on but HE HAS GONE ROUND AND TURNED EACH AND EVERY RADIATOR OFF!'

'The creep,' yelled Mrs Butler. 'The sneaky little creep! Let me at him with the bread knife!'

I continued. I talked about the bliss of when he's out for the day and, at last, you can be hot, hot, hot. But what happens when he returns? He grumbles and

pulls a face and talks about 'saunas' and 'the Tropics'
and indulges in a great deal of exaggerated fanning
and then STARTS OPENING WINDOWS!

'Ladies, there are many terrible crimes — murder,
rape, paedophilia — and this has to be up there with
them, surely?'

'He should get life!' yelled Mrs Butler. 'But can I
have a go at him with the bread knife first?'

'You may, of course, choose the non-violent route
and give him the facts,' I said. 'You may tell him that
women have a lower metabolic heat output than men,
and therefore do feel the cold more. Indeed, what is a
calorie if not a measure of heat output, and don't we
know that men burn more calories than women? You
may then wish to conclude with, "It's a physical fact,
matey. Get over it. I'm cold. The heating is on and
stays on."

'But will he accept this? No, ladies, he will not. He
will say, "Well, if you're so cold, why not put another
jumper on?" So you will say, "Well, if you're so hot,
why don't you take a jumper off?" And off it all goes
again:

1) "Put one on."
2) "Take one off."
3) "Put one on."
4) "Take one off."

5) "On."
6) "Off."
7) "On."
8) "Off."
9) "On."
10) "Off."'

I finished on a plea. 'Ladies, how are we to win this war?'

'Undetectable poisons and tampering with his brakes?' suggested Mrs Butler. 'Or even detectable poisons, what the hell?'

We considered Mrs Butler's suggestion, discussed whether we thought she might be being a bit hasty, but then concluded: No. It's the only way. It's not nice, we know, but this is what can happen to a person who is kept very, very cold . . .

Married Life

While women's magazines and suchlike always devote acres of space to advice on pepping up a long-standing marriage or relationship, little attention is ever given to those relationships that have limped on fractiously for years and years and years and will, in all likelihood, continue to do so until the end of time. Just how do you pull that kind of relationship off? This is what people are always asking us. 'NDGs,' they will say, 'how have you kept your relationship limping along fractiously for all these years?' Well, here are our top tips:

Always go to bed on an argument. That way, you can resume hostilities first thing without wasting any valuable time.

Say you'll learn the skills to be more loving, but not until you've kicked him in the shin first.

Set aside time to talk but then think, naturally enough, 'To hell with it, the all-new *ER* starts tonight.'

Arrange a night out for just the two of you somewhere nice where he will feel relaxed and comfortable, like a Women's Aid meeting.

Wear a large badge saying, 'If you think elves stack and unstack the dishwasher in the middle of the night, you are very much mistaken.' You may even want to write it on your forehead. Better still, write it on his.

Listen to his needs and then ignore them. Doesn't he realise you have enough needs of your own to think about?

Always ask him to do something while he is doing something else.

Say you *are* prepared to compromise, of course, and go along with it a bit before revealing: 'I was only joking!'

Try to understand that you are never really arguing about the 'surface' problem, even though it is fun all the same.

The Male

Always go to bed on an argument while wearing a very greasy face cream and a bath cap. This way, you can resume hostilities first thing without wasting valuable time and without having to have sex.

Help, I Haven't Even Got a Man

Women who are not in a relationship, in particular, often find Valentine's Day quite hard to stomach. As one of our founding members, Miss D. A. Ross (very much related) says: 'I know this is easy for me to say, being extremely attractive and in demand and always having to decline yet another Valentine's invitation to Venice for the weekend because, let's face it, how many Venice weekends can you go to in the one weekend? However, after a great deal of rigorous research that has nothing to do with personal experience, I do have the following advice for those who find the day rather lonely and difficult.

1) Send yourself three cards. One is a little suspicious while more than three might be overdoing it quite a bit. Make sure one card is

mushy, one is handmade and one is all sexual
innuendo, just to confirm your across-the-board
appeal, if only to yourself.

2) Always remember to disguise your handwriting on
the cards. Half the fun, after all, is trying to
figure out who your admirers might be. You may
even wish to use a post box some way from your
home, so you don't get any clues from the
postmark.

3) Tie a huge pink ribbon on whatever car happens
to be outside your home. It doesn't have to be an
especially nice car (although that helps) and it
doesn't matter who it belongs to, although you
may later have some explaining to do. All you
want is for there to be a bloody great car with a big
pink ribbon on it outside your front door. Every
so often – i.e. every two minutes – you may wish
to come into the street, gasp joyfully and then go
back inside. Your immediate neighbours will
never refer to you as 'that plain, sad old spinster'
ever again, unless, of course, it happens to be
their car, in which case you're stuffed.

4) Flowers. A single rose, delivered every hour, is
good, particularly if you work in an office. Do
check if you work in an office first, because there

is really no point in having them delivered there if you don't. Ditto chocolates and teddies.

5) Tape a note to your door saying "Have been whisked off to Venice" and then just hide behind the sofa. Remember not to answer the phone, though, as it can be a bit of a giveaway (or so it is said).

There. Sorted.'

Let's Hear It for Real Men

The following two men are the first to admit they are nothing like the usual men seen in advertisements and on television. But, just as Dove now uses 'real women' in their advertising, both men agreed to be photographed doing what real men do, and looking how most men actually look, to advertise the new Swallow range of anti-firming lotion which, if used regularly, will assist them further in not being firm about anything. 'Yes, I did say I'd fix the dripping bath tap this week but, if you recall, I was not firm about it. Plus, as you know, I have a bad back. Ouch, ouch!'

If the product is taken as recommended, users should note an increase in the number of times wives and girlfriends are prepared to Swallow such feeble excuses. (Nine out of 10 men say they notice a difference in the amount of excuses Swallowed within six weeks.) Anyway, according to the advertising agency responsible for the new campaign: 'The problem is that you see all these men on the telly such as Alan Titchmarsh and Tommy from *Ground Force* and Handy Andy from *Changing Rooms*. We all know that men aren't like this in real life, but women start to think this is how men should be even though it's a fantasy. During our extensive research down the pub and at the dogs, one man even told us that his wife once asked him: "Why can't you be more like that Laurence, who even has his own range of greeting cards now?" This, the man said, made him feel so inferior and depressed that he couldn't get up from his armchair for almost a decade, even though he usually tries to get up every eight years to tackle half-heartedly a project around the home that he'll never finish.

'Women, too, think the campaign is a good thing. Indeed, as a woman in one of our terribly focused focus groups put it: "My own partner is so woefully inadequate on the plumbing front that he can't even get the shower attachment to fit the bath taps and so always rinses his hair using an Early Learning Centre toy boat. But, having seen this campaign, I now try to laugh at him a little less cruelly. If I can."'

Here, the two men who appear in the advert, shortly to be seen on billboards throughout Europe, as well as on pizza boxes and Party Sevens, tell us why they accepted the challenge:

Chris Loughton, self-employed minicab driver, 45, divorced

'Like most men, I have the occasional bad day when I wake up and wish I was Handy Andy, even though I know it's totally unrealistic. As a teenager, in fact, I was so susceptible to images of men who could not only put up shelves, but would do so when they said they would, that I even bought myself a cordless power drill from B&Q. Needless to say, I never got it out the box, but still, how pathetically sad is that? It is very hard, though, not to buy into the fantasy, bombarded as we are by all these images of men who can and will do things round the house. It would be enough to make me turn off the telly between 8 and 9 p.m. every weekday night, but strangely never is, because then I might be asked to do something, like retrieve an item from a high shelf, which is just taking the piss at the end of the day. I should add I would have been a very hard-working minicab driver if I'd ever bothered to learn to drive. I am happy with myself and, like most men, enjoy sitting around all day sniffing my own trainers. I refuse, now, to feel bad about not being a poncey DIY star in long cuffs. I bet that Laurence doesn't Swallow. Am I divorced? I

hadn't realised. She must have left during *The Bill*.
I don't look up from *The Bill* for anybody.'

Bill Jones, unemployed, 44, tragically widowed in tragic circumstances

'I think this campaign shows once and for all that, if a
woman wants something doing, she'd better do it
herself. I'm proud to be in this campaign because it
shows men for who they are, instead of how society
thinks they should be. I've had such a positive
response from other men, who are also fed up with
women asking them to do things just because they are
either too small or too weak to do it themselves. Is
that our fault? My wife once had our bedroom
wardrobe fall on her, and because I refused to come
to her aid until I'd finished watching a very
interesting, well-researched Channel Five
programme on lap-dancing in Britain, which was
followed by an equally interesting and well-
researched programme on telephone sex in Britain
(also Channel Five, which makes some very intelligent
programmes), she never forgave me. Plus, she died.
I've yet to bury her under the patio, largely because I
haven't built it yet. I might get round to it later today,
depending on what intelligent, well-researched
programmes are being shown on Channel Five.'

A Quick Word on the Male as Father

A great dad? Let him take this test to find out:

1. Dad, your baby wakes in the night. Do you:
   a) instantly get up to comfort it;
   b) feign a deep sleep, complete with thunderous snoring;
   c) boot the mother out of bed with a 'Can't you hear the baby crying, you lazy old cow?'

2. At bedtime, do you read a story to your child:
   a) nightly;
   b) every so often;
   c) never, but offer a yummy sedative instead . . . open wide for Daddy.

3. Your child has a fever and its mother has an important meeting. Do you:
   a) volunteer to stay home;
   b) insist the mother cancels her meeting;
   c) run the thermometer under the cold tap and then exclaim, 'Look! All better! Off to school now, chop chop!'

4. An important football match is on TV but your child is nagging to go to the park. Do you:
   a) agree instantly;
   b) agree to go after the match;
   c) slip the child £20 to clear off, 'but don't tell your mother, or a monster will come in the night to bite off your nose and chop off your legs'.

5. Your daughter is wearing clothes that you consider precocious. Do you:
   a) talk to her reasonably about it;
   b) request that she changes;
   c) take a photo and post it on the internet.

6. You've been asked to assemble your child's first bed from Ikea. Do you:
   a) get to it immediately;
   b) say you will do it tomorrow;
   c) bury the Allen key at the bottom of the garden along with those 79 other Allen keys, the power drill and the 65 hammers that went strangely went missing.

7. Your partner complains (rightly) that she has to do everything round here. Do you:
   a) agree to manage your time better;
   b) agree to try to manage your time better;
   c) drag your child out by his/her collar, shouting, 'Quality time, quality time, I'll show you quality time.'

8. When your child is naughty, do you:
   a) patiently explain what the problem is;
   b) send him/her to their room;
   c) beat him/her lovingly with a hot chip pan.

9. Your son is a big ninny, cry-baby and will only wear pink. Do you
   a) love him as he is;
   b) accept he is different and special;
   c) swap him for someone else's child down the park.

10. You've missed the school play. Do you:
    a) feel terrible and apologise profusely;
    b) feel not-so terrible but still apologise profusely;
    c) get your secretary to send a fruit basket and a good bottle of wine.

Mostly a's: You're an exemplary father, but once the kids are teenagers they'll hate you all the same, so what's the point? **Mostly b's:** You try hard but are too thick to make any of it count. **Mostly c's:** You're rubbish, irresponsible and selfish and obviously haven't a clue. So, pretty average then.

So, you see, men are not as hopeless, useless, unnecessary or annoying as some people take them to be.